SOCCER

FROM BECKHAM TO ZIDANE

SOCCER

FROM BECKHAM TO ZIDANE

CHRISTOPHER MORRIS

ALADDIN PAPERBACKS
An imprint of Simon & Schuster Children's Publishing Division
1230 Avenue of the Americas, New York, NY 10020

Manufactured in China by Asia One

First Aladdin Paperbacks edition July 2008

10 9 8 7 6 5 4 3 2 1

Library of Congress Control Number 2008921758
ISBN-13: 978-1-4169-5835-2
ISBN-10: 1-4169-5835-5

Produced by
Madison Press Books
1000 Yonge Street, Suite 200
Toronto, Ontario
Canada M4W 2K2
madisonpressbooks.com

Contents

1   Soccer's Coming to North America 7

2   A World Sport 19

3   Manchester United 33

4   David Beckham 45

5   "No Hands, Please" 67

6   Fancy Kicks and Other Tricks 87

7   Women and Girls on the Field 105

8   Soccer Schools and Scholarships 115

9   Greats of the Game 123

Soccer's Coming to North America

"BANK IT LIKE BECKHAM!" said news headlines around the world in January 2007. Englishman David Beckham had just signed a new contract to play for the Los Angeles Galaxy team of Major League Soccer (MLS).

Beckham is the most famous player in the game of soccer, or *football* as it is called outside of North America. He is so well known that his name appears in the title of the popular movie *Bend It Like Beckham*, about a young soccer player who dreams of the day when she will be able to kick a ball with such skill and trickery that it bends (curves) on its way into the goal, just like David Beckham does it.

Beckham's Big Contract

The amount of money that David Beckham would "bank" with his new LA Galaxy contract was said to be more than $250 million, paid as $50 million per year for five years. This is reported to be the highest-paying contract for any professional athlete in history. Beckham is not only paid to play for the LA Galaxy, he also gets a share of the money from Galaxy ticket sales and merchandise. Even greater than all of this is the money that he is paid for the use of his name and image by large companies such as Adidas, Walt Disney, Pepsi, Gillette, and Motorola to advertise their products.

Beckham has always welcomed a challenge.
Bringing his brand of soccer to North America
may be his biggest yet.

Because Beckham will be 36 years old by the time his contract ends, which is old for a pro soccer player, some people have said that he is being paid far too much under this contract. People also thought that he was being overpaid when he signed his previous contract, with the famous Real (pronounced Rey-ahl) Madrid club of Spain. In that case, however, Beckham's contract was paid for in full before he even played one game. Within six months of his coming to the team, a million fans around the world bought the Real Madrid souvenir shirt, a copy of the one Beckham wore on the field. During his time with Real, the team earned about $500 million from these shirt sales and other off-field businesses.

Because of the size of Beckham's contract with the Los Angeles Galaxy, he had to be admitted to the league under a special rule allowing a team to sign a highly paid player in addition to their regular group of players. This arrangement is officially called the Designated Player Rule, but it soon became known as the "Beckham Rule," because he was the first player to be signed this way.

Like most professional athletes, Beckham has an agent who represents him in negotiating his contracts. Unlike many other players, though, his agent is not a former player or coach. Beckham made his deal with the LA Galaxy with the help of his good friend Simon Fuller, who is not from the world of soccer, but from the world of entertainment. Fuller is best known as the man who created the *American Idol* TV series, the highest-rated program in American television. Before this he managed several famous musicians, including the Spice Girls singing group. One of these Girls was "Posh" Spice (Victoria Adams). As Beckham said after he signed his contract with the Galaxy, "I have many reasons to be thankful to Simon Fuller, but one in particular springs to mind. He provided me with an introduction to a young lady called Victoria Adams, who went on to become Mrs. Beckham." David and Victoria were married in 1999 and have three sons: Brooklyn, Romeo, and Cruz.

Major League Soccer and the Soccer World

When David Beckham played in Spain, and before that in England, many other players in the league also earned a lot of money. Two players on the Real Madrid team, Zinedine Zidane and Ronaldo, were paid just as much as Beckham was. In Major League Soccer, on the other hand, Beckham is paid 50 times more money than the average player in the league. Most players would have to play two full years to make as much money as Beckham does for playing just one game.

Major League Soccer players are paid less than soccer players in Europe because MLS is a new league: its first games were played in 1996. Many of the famous teams in England were already more than 100 years old by that time, such as Beckham's original club Manchester United (founded in 1878), Tottenham

Beckham wears the captain's armband for his first start with the Los Angeles Galaxy.

German fans at a Women's European Cup Championship match
between the women's national teams of Germany and Belgium.

Hotspur (1882), Arsenal (1886), and Liverpool (1892). People in
England will generally root for the same team as their parents
and grandparents did. Often a new baby's first gifts will include
a tiny uniform shirt for the club that the family supports,
making the infant a fan from birth. If this favorite team's shirt is
blue, and red is the color of a hated rival team, then the family
will be sure to have blue colors all over their house, and never to
buy a red car or wear a red jacket.

Devoted fans like this can be found not only in England but
across Europe, Latin America, and many other parts of the
world. Soccer in the United States and Canada does not yet
have as many fans as in other countries. This is where "Bank

It Like Beckham" comes in. The thirteen MLS teams hope that having David Beckham in the league will bring many new fans to the game and put money in the bank for everyone, not just for him. Don Garber, the head of MLS, put it this way: "David's enormous success as a player and team leader will serve as an inspiration to millions of soccer players and fans in this country, and his global popularity will help take MLS and the sport of soccer in this country to an unprecedented level of excitement and popularity."

Tim Leiweke, president of AEG, the company that owns the Los Angeles Galaxy, said in 2005 that Beckham had "an open invitation" to join the team whenever he wanted. When this invitation was accepted, Beckham earned back the cost of his contract before he played his first game, just as he had done earlier with Real Madrid. "David has already paid for himself," Leiweke said when Beckham joined the team in July 2007. The day that Beckham arrived in Los Angeles, a new Galaxy uniform was introduced. Galaxy president Alexi Lalas reported on that day that the team had already received orders for well over 250,000 uniform shirts, before the shirt officially went on sale and before fans even knew what it would look like.

Soccer's Place in American Sports

Because soccer is so popular in other parts of the world, it is often considered a foreign sport in the United States. Actually, in terms of the number of people who play the game, it is more popular than sports we think of as very "American," such as baseball or football. Studies have shown that about 18 million Americans play soccer regularly. This is much more than the number of football or baseball players in the U.S., and second only to basketball among team sports. The number of soccer players has grown steadily over the past 20 years, while the number of people who play basketball has stayed about the same. Baseball and football have both lost popularity in terms of the number of players.

Although there are millions of Americans out on the field playing soccer, there are not as many watching it from the stands. Games in Major League Soccer draw an average of 15,000 fans per game. This is certainly a good number, and one that the MLS is happy to have. It is higher than the number of fans per game in some other countries that are famous for their love of soccer, such as Argentina or Holland.

However, it is hard not to compare soccer to other American sports, and 15,000 can seem small when it is measured against attendance for football or baseball. Teams in the National Football League attract an average 65,000 fans per game, and each Major League Baseball game draws in more than 30,000 spectators, in spite of having a long season of 162 games.

The difference in the number of people watching games on television is even greater. A very important soccer game will be watched on U.S. television in about 4 million homes, while the Super Bowl, the famous pro football championship, is seen each year in more than 60 million homes. (In fact, the Super Bowl is the most-watched program of any kind on American TV.)

No one in American soccer thinks that the sport should expect to have as many fans as football or baseball, but they may still wonder why there is such a difference between the number of people who play soccer and the number who want to watch others play it. Several reasons for this have been proposed. One idea is that there are too many other sports to watch—not only football and baseball, but also basketball, hockey, golf, auto racing, and so on. In most countries where soccer is the most popular sport, there are few other sports to attract people's attention.

Some people say they do not enjoy watching soccer because the sport does not have enough goal scoring. Professional games often end with a score of 1–0 or even 0–0. Soccer fans answer this by saying that because goals are so hard to get, it is all the more exciting when a goal is scored. They prefer this to a sport in which it is very easy to score, such as basketball, where it is not unusual for over 200 points to be scored in a game.

Dr. Henry Kissinger has a different idea. Kissinger is famous for his career in foreign affairs, especially his term as U.S. Secretary of State, during which time he won the Nobel Peace Prize. But he is also a great soccer fan who played and watched the game in his native country of Germany. He says that Americans like to watch sports that have a familiar series of set plays, like football or baseball. In soccer, the action goes on all the time without stopping, and the players have to decide on their own what to do, based on what is happening at that moment. Also, because of its continuous action and low scoring, soccer is hard to measure by numbers. As Kissinger points out, Americans love sports statistics, such as batting average or points per game, and soccer is hard to measure in this way.

More Than Just a Soccer Player

Although people have had different ideas about why soccer has not taken off in North America, they do tend to agree on the best way to make it more popular: bring over David Beckham. José Mourinho is a famous coach in Europe whose teams have won both the Premier League championship in England and the UEFA Champions League for top clubs from all over Europe. He said of Beckham, "We all in Europe want soccer in the U.S. to go up. It is a market that if it does [go up], then it is good for everybody. They couldn't choose a better player for their objectives, because he is more than a player."

In saying that David Beckham is more than a soccer player, Mourinho was referring to the fact that people everywhere know his name and recognize his picture, even though they may never have seen him play. Only two soccer players in the past have come close to this level of fame: Pelé of Brazil and Diego Maradona of Argentina. But even those two great players were famous mainly among soccer fans. Beckham appeals not only to fans but also to people who otherwise have little or no interest in soccer, or even sports in general. He is a superstar in the world at large, not just in the world of soccer.

Paul Gardner is generally considered the leading soccer writer in America and has been writing about the sport in this country for 40 years. He is not an easy man to please or impress. But after seeing Beckham play an MLS game in New York, he wrote: "Beckham's charisma needs no explaining. Here's a superstar with no sign of superiority or swagger who convinces you, very quickly, that he's still a human being like the rest of us. The smile tells it all: … It is a warm, genuine smile with a beautiful touch of boyish shyness."

Sixty-six thousand people came out to see that MLS game against the New York Red Bulls, a team that normally draws in 11,000 fans per game. So although the Red Bulls beat Beckham's Galaxy team 5–4, you could say the score that really counted was Red Bulls: 11,000 and Beckham: 55,000—fans, that is. That is what David Beckham brings to American soccer.

Beckham's first appearance in New York.

Teams in Major League Soccer

TEAM	LOCATION	STADIUM	FOUNDED
Chicago Fire	Chicago, Illinois	Toyota Park	1997
Chivas USA	Carson, California	Home Depot Center	2004
Colorado Rapids	Commerce City, Colorado	Dick's Sporting Goods Park	1995
Columbus Crew	Columbus, Ohio	Columbus Crew Stadium	1994
D.C. United	Washington, D.C.	RFK Stadium	1995
F.C. Dallas	Frisco, Texas	Pizza Hut Park	1995
F.C. Toronto	Toronto, Ontario, Canada	BMO Field	2006
Houston Dynamo	Houston, Texas	Robertson Stadium	2005
Kansas City Wizards	Kansas City, Missouri	Arrowhead Stadium	1995
Los Angeles Galaxy	Carson, California	Home Depot Center	1995
New England Revolution	Foxborough, Massachusetts	Gillette Stadium	1995
Red Bull New York (also known as the New York Red Bulls)	East Rutherford, New Jersey	Giants Stadium (The Meadowlands)	1995
Real Salt Lake	Salt Lake City, Utah	Rice-Eccles Stadium	2004

COLORS	FAN GROUP	NOTES
red and white	Section 8	Won MLS and U.S. Open Cup in their first season (1998).
red, white, and blue	Legion 1908	Parent club is the famous Mexican team Club Deportivo Guadalajara.
maroon with white and sky-blue trim	Centennial Firm	Has a working agreement with legendary English club Arsenal F.C. of London.
black and yellow	Crew Union Local 103	First team to officially join the league and also the first to have a stadium designed specifically for MLS soccer.
black and white	Screaming Eagles/ Barra Brava	First team to win both the MLS Cup and U.S. Open Cup. From 1996–1999 they were in every MLS Cup Final, winning three of them. Also won CONCACAF Champions Cup in 1998. Signed Freddy Adu at age 14.
red, white, blue, and gray	The Inferno	Formerly known as the Dallas Burn.
red, white, and gray	Red Patch Boys	First non-U.S. MLS team. Set a record by selling 14,000 season tickets before they had ever played a game.
orange and white	Texian Army/ El Batallon	Formerly the San Jose Earthquakes. Formerly Houston 1836 but Mexican fans protested the reference to Texas's war for independence. Won the MLS Cup in their first season.
blue and white	The Cauldron	Named after the Wizard of Oz.
white with blue and yellow trim	Riot Squad/ Galaxians	In 2007 added a special "red carpet" entrance to the stadium for celebrities attracted to the team by David Beckham.
blue with white and red trim	Midnight Riders	In 2007 lost the MLS Cup Final for the third year running.
white, red, and blue	Empire Supporters	Formerly known as New York/New Jersey MetroStars, then just MetroStars, now Red Bull New York after their sponsor, the popular energy drink.
red, white, blue, and yellow	The Loyalists	Have a working agreement with Spanish superclub Real Madrid.

2

A World Sport

It was the summer of 1966 and two young American tourists were enjoying their first visit to Europe. Late on a sunny afternoon at the end of July, they walked along the streets of Frankfurt, a historic city in Germany.

They were looking for a place to eat, but all the restaurants were closed. They became concerned as they walked, because the streets were empty of people and no cars went by. Then, as people began to come out of a few buildings nearby, they seemed upset, hugging each other and crying.

The two tourists asked a man who spoke English to tell them what was wrong. The man, a dignified figure in a business suit, said through his tears, "I can't even speak about it. This is the worst day for Germany since the War."

At that time, the Soviet Union faced off against the United States and other western nations in a bitter conflict known as the Cold War. Germany was at the very center of this struggle, with its huge Berlin Wall dividing East Germany from West Germany. The two worried Americans thought, "If today is the worst day for Germany since World War II, it must be that another war has started, right here."

Then they noticed a nearby newspaper stand where the owner had written in large letters on a board, "England 4, Deutschland 2." It turned out that this terrible day for Germany

English players Ray Wilson (holding trophy), Bobby Charlton (right), and Jack Charlton (behind) run the traditional "lap of honor" after winning the 1966 World Cup.

was not caused by a war, but by a soccer game. The national team of West Germany had just lost to the national team of England by a score of 4–2 in the final game of the World Cup, the championship of international soccer.

This famous game was played in the historic Wembley Stadium in London with almost 100,000 spectators looking on, including Queen Elizabeth and her husband, Prince Philip. About 400 million more people watched the game on televisions around the world. Following the game, the Queen named the coach of the winning team as a Knight of the British Empire, meaning that he would be known from then on as "Sir Alf Ramsey."

Visiting fans wave a banner offering greetings from their hometown in northern Germany.

England defender George Cohen is introduced
to Queen Elizabeth II.

"It just takes you, it holds you, it
doesn't let you go."

Wearing Your Country's Colors

The experience of those two young tourists years ago is typical of many Americans when they first realize how important the game of soccer is to people all around the world. Americans may come to recognize this when they visit a foreign country, as these women did. This can also happen right at home, when we see how much the game means to people who have come to the U.S. from other countries.

India Street is a narrow old street in the heart of San Diego, California. If you were to visit India Street during the World Cup, you would see hundreds of fans going into the Princess of Wales Pub, wearing the white shirts of England's national team with red and white face paint to match the English flag. Cross the street to the Caffe Italia, and you will see another big group of fans, this time wearing the famous shirt of the "Azzurri" (Blues), the national team of Italy. Walk on a bit, and all the shirts in another café will be green for Mexico. Then at the end of the street will be a restaurant filled with the light blue and white shirts of Argentina.

It would be very early in the morning, because California time is usually several hours earlier than where the games are being played. The fans could just as easily have stayed home in bed instead of getting up early to head off to India Street, because the games are also shown on home television. But if you are a soccer fan, it is better to watch a game in the middle of a group of shouting fans from your own country, because you know it means just as much to them as it does to you. Rene Barraza, an immigrant from Mexico, puts it this way: "It just takes you, it holds you, it doesn't

Fans celebrate Italy's victory over France in the 2006 World Cup Final.

let you go. It's my country, my blood, my flag, my people, my family, my roots, my culture. It takes hold of my country. Mexico drops everything to watch."

The World Cup of Soccer

The World Cup is played once every four years, each time in a different country. It was played in Germany in 2006 and will be held in South Africa in 2010. This will be the first time that any country in Africa has hosted the games. The United States was the host nation once in 1994, and two World Cups have been played in Mexico, in 1970 and 1986. Canada has not yet had the World Cup, but the World Cup for youth players (under age 20) was held there in 2007. This was very successful, drawing in large crowds everywhere, so Canada may be a host for the World Cup in the future.

The World Cup is relatively new compared to international soccer as a whole. The first international game was played in 1872, between England and Scotland, and the World Cup did not begin until 1930. That 1930 tournament consisted of only 13 teams, and all but two were from South America and Europe. It was not until years later

that there were enough teams from other regions that the name "World" could truly be applied to the competition.

The World Cup was the second international soccer tournament to be played. The first was the Olympic Games, which began in 1908. The people who created the World Cup wanted a new tournament because they did not think that the Olympics provided an accurate test of the abilities of a country's soccer team. Only amateurs were allowed to compete in the Olympics; that is, people who had never been paid to play the sport. Then, as now, the best players in the world were professionals, so a tournament with only amateurs would exclude many talented athletes.

The Olympic soccer tournament is held every four years, at two-year intervals with the World Cup. Though for many years the rules stated that professional players could not compete in the Olympics, they are now allowed if they are under the age of 23. There is still a lot of interest in Olympic soccer, and some games have attracted big crowds. But in terms of the effect of a soccer game on an entire nation, the Olympic soccer tournament cannot compare to the World Cup. In fact, no other sports event in the world can. The 2006 World Cup Final between Italy and France had about 715 million viewers worldwide, which was 8 times as many as the second most watched event that year, the Super Bowl.

Playing in the World Cup

Any country in the world may enter its national team in the World Cup competition. In fact, it is said that the first thing that a nation does when it becomes independent is to design its own flag. The second is to form a national soccer team. Some national groups have soccer teams even though they are not officially recognized as countries, such as the Basque and Catalonia regions of Spain and the Palestinian territory of the Middle East.

There is another connection between a country's flag and its soccer team: the colors of the team's uniform are often taken from the colors of its country's flag. Thus, teams from Ireland and Nigeria wear green, Brazil and Sweden wear gold and blue, and Canada, Chile, China, Denmark, and Turkey are among the many countries that wear red. The United States usually wears white uniforms with a red and blue trim.

Each country picks an "all-star" team of its best players to compete for the World Cup. For two years before the actual World Cup, all countries play in tournaments in their own regions, and the top teams in those tournaments go on to the Cup itself. Thirty-two teams in all qualify for the World Cup, from six different regions: Africa, Asia, Europe, North and Central America, Oceania (nations of the western Pacific), and South America. Europe and South America will have the most teams in the tournament, because they have each won the World Cup nine times and no other region has ever won. Brazil has the most World Cup titles with five, Italy has won four times, Germany three, Uruguay and Argentina twice each, and England and France once each.

A 2006 research project called the Big Count made a survey of all the soccer-playing nations in the world to find out how many people play the game worldwide. According to this study, there are about 265 million soccer players in the world. Asia has the most of any continent with 85 million, followed by Europe with 62 million, and Africa with 46 million. Among individual countries, China has the most total players, followed by the U.S., India, Germany, and Brazil. The U.S. also has the most youth players, and Germany has the most who play in official leagues. Brazil has by far the most professional players.

Different Lands, Different Styles

Soccer is played all over the world, and the Laws (rules) of the game are the same everywhere. As you might expect, though, different countries around the globe play the game in different ways. These differences come from many factors, such as the history of the game in a certain country, the typical weather and field conditions there, and the character and culture of the people.

For example, games in England are often played in cool weather on damp fields, and English teams are known for doing a lot of hard running during a game and trying to get the ball by sliding along the wet ground. Players pass the ball over long distances, and being able to play the ball with your head is very important.

In Latin America, games are more likely to be played in hot weather on a hard, dry field. In these conditions, there is not as much running up and down the field as there is in the English game, and players like to move the ball with a series of short, quick passes rather than one long one. For Latin American teams like Argentina, Mexico, or Uruguay, more of the game is played with the ball on the ground, rather than in the air as in England.

There are two famous playing styles of Europe that are quite different from each other. Italy became known for a style called *catenaccio*, which means "the big chain." The idea is that a chain of defensive players stretches all the way across the field to stop the other team from scoring. Holland, a small country in terms of population and area, has produced many great players who play a style known as "Total Football." In Total Football, each player on the team is expected to be good at all parts of the game, not just at one or two things based on the position he plays.

The United States does not (yet) have a distinct playing style the way other countries do. This is probably because the players come from so many different backgrounds. The team often has players

A player celebrates a goal by raising his shirt over his head.

who were not born in the U.S., or whose parents were not born here. Also, there is no single type of weather or field condition that is typical for the sport throughout the country.

Samba Soccer

Fans from different countries will support the style in which their own national team plays, of course, but people generally agree as to which country has the best style: Brazil. The Brazilian style is called by different names, such as "the football of the sun," *Joga Bonito* (the Beautiful Game), or the *samba*. The samba is the national dance of Brazil, and when the Brazil team is playing at its best, it can look like they are turning, twisting, and spinning to the rhythm of samba music.

When a player from another country plays in a creative style that is a joy to watch, the highest compliment for this is to say he is "like a Brazilian." When the Total Football of Holland became famous in the 1970s, the players began to be called "the Brazilians of Europe."

Like kings and queens, the great Brazilian players are known by just one name: Garrincha, Didi, Zico, Socrates, Romario, Ronaldo, Kaka. The greatest Brazilian player of them all, Pelé, was in effect elevated to royal status, and was known as King Pelé.

The Brazilian style is built on a foundation of great skill. It does not matter how many tricks a player can do with the ball if he cannot control the ball in the first place. When a great Brazilian player like Ronaldinho receives a long pass from the other side of the field, he will stop the ball in an instant without letting it bounce away, managing it as easily as if it were a soft pillow rather than a hard ball. Then he will run with the ball so that it seems glued to his foot, going past one opposing player after another.

There is more to samba soccer than skill, though. You might be watching a Brazilian team on TV and nothing special will be happening. But don't go to get a snack from the fridge just yet, because when you least expect it, Brazil will suddenly fool the other team and score a great goal. This may be on a long kick far away from goal, or on a quick shot right in front of the net, or, best of all, at the end of a series of short passes from one player to the next. However it happens, you'll be glad you stayed in your seat to watch, because this is the Beautiful Game.

Pelé takes a shot on goal in the 1962 World Cup.

3

Manchester United

Manchester is a large city in northwestern England. It is described as the city where Europe's great Industrial Revolution began in the late 1700s. The city built factories to produce clothing and other products from cotton, and canals and railroads to carry these goods to other places for sale. However, Manchester's most famous product today is not clothing, but soccer players. The city is home to Manchester United, the leading soccer club in the world.

"Come On, You Reds"

Manchester United's nickname is "the Reds," from the famous bright red color of their uniform shirts. Today United fans can be seen wearing these red shirts on the streets of nearly every big city in the world, even in countries where the team rarely plays, such as the United States, South Africa, India, and China. The team is said to have at least 75 million fans worldwide, more than any other team in any sport.

A good measure of a team's popularity is the traffic at their official website. In March of 2007 United attracted 2.2 million unique visitors to its website, making it the world's most popular soccer club online. About 60% of these visitors live outside of Great Britain, showing the global appeal of the Manchester United brand. And this does not even count the visitors to the team's many unofficial websites, such as "Totally Red" or "United We Stand."

Manchester United players celebrate a goal.

Manchester United has won the championship of English soccer 16 times. They have also won the Football Association (FA) Cup 11 times, the most of any team. The FA Cup is a "knock-out" tournament, meaning that the loser of a game is kicked out of the competition while the winner continues. Any team in England can play in it, professional or amateur, and over 600 teams will enter the FA Cup in a typical year.

As a business, Manchester United has a current value of almost $1.5 billion. This is about $450 million greater than the second richest soccer team, Real Madrid of Spain, and it makes United one of the two most valuable sports teams in the world, along with the Dallas Cowboys of the NFL, who are the richest team in North America. In comparison, the New York Yankees are the most valuable baseball team at $1.2 billion, the New York Knicks head the list in basketball at $600 million, and the Toronto Maple Leafs are tops in hockey at $335 million. The biggest expense for a sports business like Manchester United is the money paid to the players. United's highest-paid players at the present time are reported to earn more than $200,000 a week.

The "Heathens" Become Manchester United

Manchester United Football Club goes back to the year 1878. The original name of the team was not Manchester United but Newton Heath LYR. A group of men who worked at the Lancashire and Yorkshire Railway yards in Manchester got together to form the team, and they played games against teams from other railroad companies in the Lancashire area. They were known as "the Heathens," from the name "Heath."

At that time, soccer teams were made up of friends who had gone to the same university, or who worked together in the same factory or business, like these railroad workers. They played soccer for fun rather than for pay. It is said that the first time a professional player played for the England national team, he had to wear a different color shirt than the other players to show that he was being paid to play. (He was paid the grand sum of £1, or about $2.00.)

The Newton Heath club never had much money, and in the early 1900s it looked like they might go out of business. The club was rescued by John Henry Davies, who used money from his successful beer business, the Manchester Brewery Company, to finance the team. The story is told that Davies learned about the Newton Heath team when he found a lost St. Bernard dog that belonged to team captain Harry Stafford.

By this time the name "Newton Heath" no longer fit the team, because the players came from many different places rather than just the railroad company. The team wanted a new name to show that they represented the whole city of Manchester, and so "Manchester United" was chosen in the spring of 1902.

The Manchester United team lines up before its match against Red Star Belgrade of Yugoslavia on February 6, 1958.

Following page: Ground and aerial views of Manchester United's Old Trafford playing field.

Old Trafford, the Theater of Dreams

The most famous name associated with the club, aside from the team name itself, is "Old Trafford." This is the stadium where the team has played its games since 1910. John Henry Davies and his brewery company paid for the land and the building work for the Old Trafford stadium. Old Trafford has changed many times since it was built, but the stadium has always remained in the same place, south of the Manchester Ship Canal.

During World War II the city of Manchester was a major target for German bombers, and in March 1941 the Germans attacked the Trafford Park industrial area. Bombs hit Old Trafford hard, landing right on the playing field and destroying one of the main stands. It was not until 1949 that Old Trafford was completely rebuilt and able to be used again for games.

Today Old Trafford is known as the "Theater of Dreams" because of the many dramatic and memorable games that have been played there. The current stadium holds about 76,000 people, making it one of the largest soccer stadiums in the world. The club reports that more than 200,000 fans each year visit Old Trafford when the team is not there, just to see the stadium and visit the club museum.

"Glory, Glory Man United"

The area behind one goal at Old Trafford has long been known as the Stretford End. In the original stadium there were no seats there, and fans would stand crowded together. The Stretford End became known as the place where United's most dedicated and loudest fans could be found. It is said that the noise levels from the Stretford End crowd were measured and found to be louder than the sound of a jet airliner taking off.

Americans would probably expect a lot of noise from the crowd at a Manchester United game, because American football also draws big, noisy crowds. What they might be surprised to hear, though, is that United fans not only like to cheer for their team, they also like to sing. Certain sections of the crowd at Old Trafford will sing for almost the entire game, and songs are sure to be heard after a United player has scored a goal or made a good play. The songs are not planned and there is no official song leader. A group of fans will just take up a song, typically in the Stretford End, and then others in the stadium will join in.

The favorite team song is probably "Glory, Glory Man United," to the tune of the famous American Civil War song "Glory, Glory Hallelujah." The fans, though English, often base their singing on American popular songs, such as "Oh, When the Reds Go Marching In" from "When the Saints Go Marching In" or "I See the Stretford End A-rising" from "Bad Moon Rising." A favorite player, Ole Gunnar Solskjaer (pronounced by fans as o-lee shole-shire), was serenaded with the country music song "You Are My Sunshine:" "You are my Solskjaer, my Ole Solskjaer, you make me happy, when skies are gray." United fans even like to make fun of the favorite songs of rival teams, like when they sing "You'll Never Get a Job" to the tune of "You'll Never Walk Alone," the theme song of Liverpool F.C.

United fans around the world buy recordings of the team's songs. One of the most popular of these is the CD *Come On You Reds*, which includes favorites such as "George Best, Belfast Boy," "Ooh Aah Cantona," and "Ryan Giggs, We Love You." The album cover has images of Best, Cantona, Giggs, and other famous United players, standing together just like the figures on the cover of the Beatles' classic Sgt. Pepper's album.

The Busby Babes

England's national soccer league, the Football League, was called off during World War II, and play did not resume until 1946. At that time the fortunes of Manchester United were low. The team had always had a lot of fans, but until that time they had not had great success on the field. They had been part of the Football League for more than 60 years but had only won the League twice, the more recent of those titles coming in 1911. In the

Manchester United players celebrate after winning the 1967 Football League Championship. From left, Bobby Charlton, Denis Law (with trophy), George Best and Billy Foulkes.

previous 40 years the team had never finished higher than ninth place in the Football League, and for most of the 1930s United did not even play in the League's top division.

This all changed when a Scotsman named Matt Busby was made manager of the team for the 1946–47 season. Since then, United has almost always been among the best teams in England. In Busby's first year the team finished second in the League, and they went on to finish second several more times before winning the championship in 1952. They won five championships in all under Busby, and also won the FA Cup twice.

The biggest change Matt Busby brought to the team was that he was always ready to try out a young player who had not yet proved himself as part of the regular team. He was famous for saying, "If they are good enough, they are old enough." His group of young players became known as the "Busby Babes," and they were some of the best players in the country. The greatest of the Babes, Duncan Edwards, was only 16 years old when he played his first game for United.

The Munich Crash

In 1958 Manchester United played in a tournament called the European Cup. It was similar to the English FA Cup, but included teams from all over Europe. The championship team from each soccer league in Europe could enter the European Cup.

The United team was led by captain Roger Byrne, who also played for the English national team. Busby Babe Duncan Edwards was only 21, but was already thought of as the best all-around player England had ever produced. Two other stars were Tommy Taylor, a tall forward with an outstanding ability to head the ball, and Bobby Charlton, known for his powerful shooting from long distances.

On February 6, 1958, the United team was at an airport in Munich, Germany. They were on their way back to Manchester from a European Cup game against Red Star Belgrade of Yugoslavia. It was a snowy day and the runway was covered with slush. Their plane tried twice to take off but could not get up into the air. Finally on the third try it seemed that the plane would be able to take off, but then it lost height and struck a fence at the end of the runway. The plane then skidded along the frozen ground and crashed into a house.

Twenty-three of the 44 people on board the plane died. Roger Byrne, Tommy Taylor, and five other United players were killed instantly. Duncan Edwards survived, but with terrible injuries. He died in a hospital after fighting for his life for two weeks. Manager Matt Busby was also severely injured and at one point was not expected to live. Among the players who escaped death, two never played again and several others could not recover the abilities they had before the crash. Bobby Charlton was pulled away from the wreckage by a teammate, goalkeeper Harry Gregg.

Although Charlton was not badly hurt and was able to resume playing, he was affected mentally by what he had experienced, and it was some time before he returned to top form.

At the entrance to Old Trafford stands the famous Munich Clock. It bears the single word "Munich" and the date, February 6, 1958. It still keeps time, but it is said that on one anniversary of the crash, the hands of the clock stopped at 3:04 PM, the exact time that the plane went down.

Rebuilding from the Ruins

After losing so many players in the Munich crash, the future was uncertain for United. Many people felt that the team would have to play in a lower league for a time, or possibly even stop playing altogether. However, Matt Busby recovered from his injuries, and he soon began to rebuild the team with new players.

Denis Law and George Best were the best of these new players. Law was a Scottish forward with a great ability to score important goals. He was known as "the King of the Stretford End" because he was so popular with the fans there. Best was a colorful and unpredictable player from Belfast, Northern Ireland. The scout who spotted him there immediately sent a message to Busby saying, "I think I've found you a genius."

Best was especially known for his ability to control the ball and dribble past defenders. He also had great speed and balance, could run hard for an entire game, could play the ball with either foot, was dangerous anywhere near goal, could head the ball well, and would even come back to help on defense!

Best and Law joined Bobby Charlton, who was now back on the field and playing at his best again. Each of these three would go on to win the award given each year to the best player in all of Europe. Led by the Best-Charlton-Law trio, United returned to the European Cup and in 1968 they won it, becoming the first English team to do so.

A Team for the World

The tragedy of the Munich crash, combined with the success of the Best-Charlton-Law team, attracted a large number of fans from outside Manchester, including Ted Beckham and his son David, who lived in East London. David said of his father, "He had already been following United, but [the Munich crash] turned it into a lifelong obsession for him."

Then in the 1990s, a whole new group of recruits joined Manchester United's Red Army. These were fans from all over the world who came to know the team from watching televised games of the English Premier League. The 20 best teams in the country play in this league, which was formed in 1992. At the time of publication, Manchester United had won the Premier League nine times. This is more than all other teams put together, and only three other teams have won the championship even once. In every year that United did not win, they finished either second or third.

Not only did United win the Premier League nine times, they won with style. Though many teams in soccer today put defense first and offense second, the approach of United manager Alex Ferguson has always been to play free-flowing, attacking soccer, especially at Old Trafford. From the time of United's first Premier League championship team with Eric Cantona, they have featured players who could score or set up goals. This is still true today as the two best young players in England, Cristiano Ronaldo and Wayne Rooney, both wear the red shirt of Manchester United.

4

David Beckham

"That moment was the start of it all: the attention, the press coverage, the fame, that whole side of what's happened to me since. . . . When my foot struck that ball, it kicked open the door to the rest of my life." This is what David Beckham wrote about the most famous goal of his career, a shot that he made in the first game of the season in August 1996.

Manchester United had an away game in South London that day against Wimbledon Football Club. In the second half, David took a pass from a teammate in the middle of the field. He was more than 60 yards from the goal, and no player is supposed to shoot from that far away. But David had the sense that he might be able to fool the goalkeeper with a long shot, and he thought, "Why not?" The ball left his right foot exactly at the halfway line and flew high in the air. It seemed to be going wide at first, but it had the now-famous Beckham "bend" on it, and it curled back toward the goal. Goalkeeper Neil Sullivan realized the danger and scrambled to get back, but it was too late. The ball sailed over his head and into the net as the commentator shouted, "What an astonishing goal!"

David Beckham had always loved soccer, and his talent had been obvious to others from his youth. But this was the moment when his life took off for new heights, like that shot flying up into the summer sky.

Beckham scores for England with a penalty kick
in a 2002 World Cup game against Argentina.

A young Beckham poses with Terry Venables.

Born to Bend It

David grew up in a part of East London called Chingford with his father, Ted, mother, Sandra, older sister, Lynne, and little sister, Joanne. His father played soccer for a local team and he passed on his love of the game to David. He would bring David to his games, and even let the boy play in practice games with the men's team. David also spent as many hours as he could playing with boys his age and a bit older at Chase Lane Park near his house.

By the time David was eight years old, his father could see he was developing into something special, and he decided to give up his own regular playing so that he could concentrate on helping David. Others had also heard about David playing at Chase Lane Park, and he was invited to join a new youth team called Ridgeway Rovers. They became one of the top youth teams in the area, and David also began to play for his school and for special select teams representing his area and his county. By the time he was 11, professional clubs in London had begun to ask about him and started to attend his Ridgeway Rover games.

David really caught people's attention when he entered a soccer skills competition, whose sponsor, Bobby Charlton, was one of the greatest players in the history of the English game.

From left, Nicky Butt, Ryan Giggs, David Beckham, and Gary Neville.

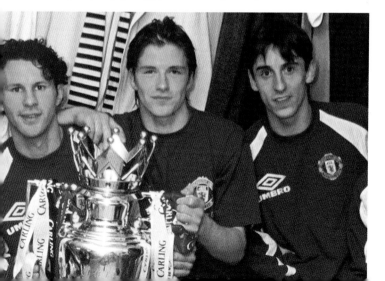

"I'd like to think about it, Mr. Venables."

The Charlton competition called for boys to show their skill in kicking and controlling the ball, short and long passing, dribbling, juggling, and so on. The prize for winning was a free trip to Spain to meet the world-famous Barcelona soccer team. David made it through to the finals of the competition, which were held at Manchester United's Old Trafford stadium. In front of a crowd of about 40,000 people, who were there to see United's game that day, David won the contest. The boy in second place was 15 years old, and the third-place finisher was 19. David Beckham, the winner, was only 10.

United It Will Be

Before Beckham joined Manchester United, he was part of the training program at another big club called Tottenham Hotspur. Their historic White Hart Lane stadium was only 15 minutes from his home, and his grandfather was a big fan of the Spurs team and went to all their games.

At the age of 12 Beckham was called to the Spurs offices at the Lane to meet with team manager Terry Venables. He offered Beckham a good contract to join the team, but David was disappointed that Mr. Venables did not seem to know who he was. Not only had they met before, during David's prize trip to Barcelona, but he had been training at the Spurs team facility for several years. He also kept in mind that his real dream had always been to play for Manchester United. So he thought for a moment and then answered, "I'd like to think about it, Mr. Venables."

David and his parents then drove up to Manchester to meet with United team officials. It was May 2, 1988, his birthday. In English soccer, players can become part of a club's youth program even when they are as young as 13. If the club is in another city, as United was for David, then players will move in with a family in that city. So, on the ride from London to Manchester, David and his parents were thinking about the fact that if he chose United over Spurs, he would be leaving home at a young age.

David knew that his father's favorite team was Manchester United, but on the other hand, he sensed that his mother would want him to sign with Spurs, so that he could continue to live at home. But neither one put pressure on him; they left the decision up to him. When the Beckhams arrived at United's headquarters, manager Alex Ferguson was there to meet them himself. Mr. Ferguson not only knew who David was, he knew all about his family as well. The team even knew it was David's birthday and had a cake ready for him.

The Beckhams watched United play that afternoon and then went up to Mr. Ferguson's office. The meeting was short and simple. Ferguson said, "We'd like to give you two, two, and two." This meant that United would sign David for six years: two years as a schoolboy player, two years with the team's Youth Training Scheme, and two years as a full professional. This was the same six-year offer he had received earlier from Tottenham. David did not need to hear any more. "I want to sign," he said.

Fergie's Fledglings

David Beckham moved to Manchester permanently when he was 15 years old. United had arranged to have boys from other cities stay with local people who had a connection to the team. David enjoyed living with a family named the Kays, who lived right next door to the United training grounds.

In the United youth team David found himself part of an outstanding group of players, including the Neville brothers, Gary and Phil, who were solid defenders. Midfielder Nicky Butt was known for hard work and crunching tackles, and red-headed Paul Scholes did not look like a top player at first, but he had a knack for both scoring goals and setting them up for others. These players were all David's age. Just a bit older was another boy named Ryan Giggs, who stood out above them all for his speed and dribbling ability.

As a new arrival from London, Beckham had to get to know these boys, who had grown up in the Manchester area and had known each other for some time. At first, they thought of him as "a flashy little Cockney," because of the way he dressed, and they enjoyed making fun of his strong Cockney (East London) accent. Ryan Giggs said, "We're always imitating him, but he doesn't mind, he just laughs."

This group of young players would go on to become stars for Manchester United and play for the English national team (or the Welsh team in the case of Giggs). When manager Alex Ferguson brought these players into the senior team, they became known as "Fergie's Fledglings," a fledgling being a young bird just learning to fly on its own. This was a play on the name of a previous group of outstanding young players produced by the United youth system, the Busby Babes of the 1950s. The soccer world first learned of Fergie's Fledglings when the team won the FA Youth Cup, the equivalent of the famous FA Cup for young players.

Heading North to Preston North End

When David was 17, he got his first chance to play for the United senior team. He was called into the squad that would play against Brighton in a League Cup tournament game. He was sitting on the bench with about 20 minutes left to play, when Ferguson told him to get ready to go into the game. David was so excited to hear this that he jumped off the bench and banged his head on the top of the dugout.

Though David did all right in this game, it did not lead to chances for more playing time. Over the next two years he played in a few more games, and even scored his first goal for the team. But he saw that some of the other Fledgings were advancing at a faster pace. Ryan Giggs was already an important part of the senior team, and others such as Gary Neville were also getting chances to play. David began to doubt that he would ever be good enough to be a first-team player for United, and what happened next really made him worry.

One day after practice, Alex Ferguson called David into his office and said, "Preston North End have asked if they could take you on loan for a month. I think it's a good idea." Preston North End had a long history and had once been the best team in England, but that was many years earlier and they now played in a lower league. David would be leaving the top club in the country to go to a far less important team.

At first David thought that United no longer wanted him, and that being sent to Preston was their first step in getting rid of him entirely. He was also nervous about joining a new team, afraid that the other Preston players would think he had a high opinion of himself because he was from Manchester United. He was disappointed to see how little money the Preston club had to spend on the team. However, David was determined to make the best of the situation and move forward. He worked hard in games and in practice, and the other Preston players accepted him.

David came to realize that he had been sent out to Preston so that he could work on the physical part of his game—playing through hard tackles from opposing players, and getting in good tackles himself. There was no doubt about his ability to control and kick the ball. But, at Preston, he also became a tougher player who was more comfortable in the aggressive and physical aspects of the game. When David's time at Preston was supposed to end, his attitude toward the team had changed so much that he asked if he could stay there longer. Alex Ferguson's answer was "No." United had other plans for David in the coming year.

"You'll win nothing with kids." So said Alan Hansen, a former star player who had become a television commentator at the start of the 1995–96 season. He was referring to the decision by Alex Ferguson to bring a whole group of new young players into the Manchester United starting lineup, including the Neville brothers, Paul Scholes, Nicky Butt, and David Beckham. Hansen's prediction turned out to be quite wrong, as this young team went on to win what is called "the Double." The Double is the exceptional achievement of winning the Football League and the FA Cup tournament in the same season. In the past 100 years, United is one of only four teams to have done this.

World Cup 1998

When Glenn Hoddle became manager of the English national team, David Beckham got his first chance to play for his country. Hoddle had been a great player himself and his playing style was similar to Beckham's, with outstanding ball skills and a great ability to deliver long passes.

Beckham became a regular member of England's team in the games leading up to the 1998 World Cup in France, so he was surprised when he was not included in the lineup for the first game of the World Cup itself. Hoddle told him that he was left out because he did not seem to be focused enough on soccer, something that would also cause problems with Alex Ferguson later in his career.

One of England's starting players was hurt in the second World Cup game, so David did get to play, and in the third game he played again and scored a goal. Then came a game against Argentina, a bitter rival of England's ever since the two nations had fought each other in the Falklands War of 1982.

The game was even at 2–2 in the second half when David was knocked to the ground by Argentine player Diego Simeone. Referee Kim Milton Nielsen of Denmark rushed over to call a foul on Simeone. It then appeared that Simeone teased Beckham or pulled at his hair. Beckham made the mistake of reacting to this, and kicked up at Simeone from the ground. Referee Nielsen was on the scene and he immediately showed the red card, sending Beckham off the field.

Beckham holds the FA Cup after Manchester United beat Newcastle 2–0 in 1999.

Beckham is sent off the field by referee Kim
Milton Nielsen after kicking at Argentina's
Diego Simeone (below, center), during
a 1998 World Cup match.

England eventually lost the game in a penalty kick shoot-out, and they were out of the World Cup. Afterward, Hoddle said that if the game had been played as 11 players against 11, England would have won. People took this to mean that the loss was Beckham's fault, and the English press and fans attacked Beckham. Newspapers shouted out headlines such as "Ten Heroic Lions, One Stupid Boy."

Although he was being criticized in the rest of the country, Beckham was encouraged by the support he got from Alex Ferguson and the Manchester United fans. Only one England player had talked to Beckham in the dressing room after the Argentina loss, but that player's words stayed with him. Tony Adams, a veteran player, had said to him, "You can be stronger for this. You can be a better player for it." David would become just that.

Three Trophies in One Year

During the following season, David was not popular with the fans at visiting stadiums. He had to face boos, insults, and even threats, but he put up with this and concentrated on his job with Manchester United. He also had the happy news that he was about to become a father, and this helped him put the Argentina game behind him.

In the 1998–99 season, United won the Double again, and this time they went one better by making it a Treble (Triple), something that no English team had ever done before. They won the Football League, the FA Cup, and then followed this by beating Bayern Munich of Germany to win the European Cup. Bayern led 1–0 for almost the entire game, but at the very end United scored twice within a minute to win the match. Both goals were scored by Beckham, who shot two corner kicks perfectly into the goal area.

Beckham continued to play for England and eventually became captain of the team. As time went on, he won over the England fans who had booed him earlier. This became obvious in October 2001 in a home game against Greece. The entire stadium cheered wildly for him when he scored with one of his curving free kicks to give England the result they needed to qualify for the 2002 World Cup.

The United Years Come to an End

Ever since he had joined Manchester United at age 13, David believed that manager Alex Ferguson respected him and thought him committed to the team. As the years went on, though, the relationship began to change. David felt that Ferguson was treating him in a cold, unfriendly way. David has written that when he asked what the problem was, Ferguson told him that he no longer seemed to be loyal enough to the Manchester United club. In Alex Ferguson's opinion, a United player should think of the club first, last, and always, and nothing should distract him from it.

David played not only for United but also for the England national team. He was also very committed to his family, and wanted to be able to spend time with them whenever possible. Beyond this there was the matter of David Beckham the famous celebrity, whose picture now appeared constantly in the fashion and entertainment sections of newspapers, as well as on the sports page. Alex Ferguson had grown up in a tough shipyard district in Glasgow, Scotland, a far cry from the London celebrity circles in which David and his wife now moved.

"There was a chill in the air between the two of us," Beckham said, but one day in February of 2003 this chill turned red hot. The United team had just returned to its locker room after losing a game at home to rival club Arsenal. According to

"...a United player should think of the club first, last, and always, and nothing should distract him."

David, he became upset when Ferguson blamed him for a mistake that caused an Arsenal goal. He argued back by saying the goal was not his fault, and then he swore at the manager—something that a United player should never, ever do. Ferguson was so angry at this that he kicked at a soccer shoe which was lying on the floor. The shoe flew up in the air and hit David in the face, cutting him over his eye. He charged toward Ferguson as if to fight with him, though his teammates stopped him. Both men calmed down, but, from then on, David Beckham's days at Manchester United were numbered.

A New Star for the Galácticos

At the present time there is only one other club in the world that is as big as Manchester United, and that is Real Madrid of Spain. The most important trophy in club soccer is the European Cup, and Real Madrid has won this nine times, more than any other team. So when Beckham realized he would have to leave United, Real Madrid was the only team he wanted to join.

At Real Madrid Beckham became one of a group of famous players known as the Galácticos (superstars), along with Zinedine Zidane of France, Luis Figo of Portugal, Raul of Spain, and Roberto Carlos and Ronaldo of Brazil. At Manchester United David's shirt number had been 7, but at Real Madrid the #7 shirt was already taken; it was worn by Raul, who had been with the team since the age of 15. David decided to take shirt #23, in honor of the great basketball player Michael Jordan, who wore this number with the Chicago Bulls. David continues to wear #23 with his current team, the Los Angeles Galaxy.

In spite of all the great players on the team, Real Madrid had a hard time winning trophies during David's time there. They did not win the Spanish Cup or the European Cup, and they were second in La Liga (the Spanish League) during his first two years with the team. Although the Galácticos could all work magic with the ball, the team was short of hard-working players who could stop the other team from scoring.

From the Galácticos to the Galaxy

At the beginning of 2007 David's Real Madrid career was at a low point. He was not getting much playing time, and his contract with the team was coming to an end. When he announced that he was leaving Madrid to sign with the Los Angeles Galaxy, the Real coach said that Beckham would not play in any of their games for the rest of the season. To make matters worse, he had also been dropped from the English national team by new coach Steve McClaren. It looked like Beckham would spend several months on the sidelines waiting for his Galaxy contract to begin in July.

Just as he did before when he overcame the setbacks of being loaned to Preston North End and being sent off in the World Cup, Beckham faced this difficult time by working hard, keeping a professional attitude, and doing his best on the field. He not only got back into the Real Madrid lineup, but played very well and helped the team to win the La Liga. The English team had struggled without him, and in May he was called back to that team as well. He immediately showed that he deserved the honor as he used

Beckham, wearing the LA Galaxy uniform.

his trademark long passes to set up three goals in his first two games back.

In his current role with the Galaxy, and as the man in the spotlight for American soccer in general, Beckham faces a new and different challenge. Based on his past career, he has what it takes to meet this challenge.

Beckham the Superstar

By the time he reached his mid-20s, David Beckham had achieved the soccer dreams of his boyhood. He had become a professional player for his favorite club, Manchester United, and he had been chosen for the English national team. As a famous player for England, Beckham shared the spotlight with others, such as the midfield genius Paul Gascoigne, defender Tony Adams, and top goal scorers Michael Owen and Alan Shearer. Toward the end of the 1990s Beckham moved beyond those players, beyond all others in the sport, and into a different world.

From Fan to Close Friend

In November 1996, David Beckham was sitting in a hotel room in the nation of Georgia in Eastern Europe, talking with his friend Gary Neville. The television was showing a music video of the Spice Girls, a popular English singing group made up of five young women. The one who caught his eye was "Posh" Spice. (*Posh* is a British word meaning "fancy" or "high-class.") He said to Neville, "She's so beautiful. I just love everything about her. I've got to meet her. That's the girl I'm going to marry."

David and Posh (Victoria Adams) did meet, and they found out that they had grown up near each other in London. They began to spend time together, and on one of their first dates they went to see the movie *Jerry Maguire*, starring Tom Cruise. Just ten years later, David and Victoria, now Mr. and Mrs. Beckham, would see Tom Cruise in a very different setting. The Beckhams became close friends with Cruise and his wife, Katie Holmes.

Just three of Beckham's
many hairstyles.

When Beckham joined the Galaxy, Cruise hosted a grand party welcoming the Beckhams to Los Angeles.

An English soccer player had become so famous that he formed a friendship with the world's top-ranking movie star. Books about his life topped the bestseller lists, and his face was seen on hundreds of magazine covers, even magazines for women that had never before featured an athlete. This says much about David Beckham and the modern culture of superstar celebrities.

The Beckham Style

David Beckham always had a sense of style, even as a boy. When he visited Manchester United to sign his first professional contract, he was dressed up in a special blue blazer and a fancy red United tie. His hair was worn in a "spiky" style that he thought made him look like Gordon Strachan, one of United's top players at the time. When he joined United's youth team shortly after this, the other boys noticed right away that he would always have the sharpest-looking uniform and soccer boots (shoes).

Today Beckham wears a special soccer boot called the David Beckham Predator Pulse, which was designed exclusively for him and which has a store price of over $200. If you wanted to buy a pair of boots that David had actually worn, though, that would cost you a bit more. The auction house Christie's reported that a buyer paid about $28,000 for such a pair in 2006. Beckham's actual game-worn shirts can bring a price of $1,500 to $5,000.

The "Strachan spike" may have been Beckham's first distinctive hairstyle, but it would not be the last. Just as some people watch to see what he will do with the soccer ball, others watch to see what he will do with his hair. At any given time it could be dark brown, blond, or streaked blond. It might be shoulder length, medium length, or a buzz cut. It could be in the form of a Mohawk, half Mohawk, or mullet, or arranged in corn rows. Whatever the style, it will be paired with one of the fashionable styles worn by Victoria, such as her current "Pob" (Posh bob).

The camera loves David Beckham and photographers love to get his picture. He looks good in any photo, no matter what the setting or how the picture was taken. He is like a movie star and the public is fascinated by him. Each time he appears in public, he is likely to sport a different look or style in terms of clothing and hair.

The Beckham Family

The marriage of "Posh" and "Becks" in 1999 was the biggest celebrity wedding in Britain since Prince Charles married Lady Diana Spencer in 1981. It was only fitting, then, that David and Victoria were married in a royal setting, at Luttrellstown Castle outside Dublin, Ireland. The bride wore white, and so did the groom: an elegant white suit with matching tie and shoes, designed by London tailor Timothy Everest. After the ceremony, the couple changed into matching purple outfits for the wedding dinner.

David was now not only a celebrity himself, but the husband of a famous pop singer. The couple's three sons have also become familiar to the public: Brooklyn (age eight as of this publication); Romeo (five), and Cruz (two). David is more than a star athlete, he is the husband of a glamorous woman, the father of three good-looking boys, a fashion leader in dress and hair style, and even a bit of a rebel spirit through his many tattoos. Among these tattoos are the names of his wife and children, the Roman numeral VII (seven) for his England uniform number, a Christian cross, and a guardian angel.

"Becks" and "Posh" at the 2003 MTV Movie Awards in Los Angeles.

Right: Wax figures of David and Victoria Beckham are displayed at Madame Tussaud's Museum in New York City.

The Beckham Brand

The Beckham image is one of youth, talent, fitness, and general all-around star power. This appeals to young people around the world, both male and female, and many companies will hire him when they want consumers to associate his image with their business and their products. He is especially popular with companies that promote their brand in Asia, even though he has played there only a few times.

As one would expect, these products include clothing and hair care items. They also include shaving products, soft drinks, candy bars, and mobile phones. He even has had his own line of clothing, called "Seven" after his uniform number. His biggest deal is with Adidas, a giant German company that makes soccer uniforms and other sports equipment. His Adidas contract is said to be the largest of any athlete in history, and it is reported that he sells more products on his own than all other Adidas clients combined.

The Beckham brand has become so prominent that a person can earn a living by serving as a discount version of this, so to speak. Englishman Paul Mansley acts as a Beckham double who looks and sounds just like him and can even do some of his tricks with the soccer ball. Mansley works in films and TV shows, and his talent agency sometimes pairs him with a "wife," a woman who is a look-alike for Victoria Beckham.

Beckham's rise to the top of the celebrity world was fueled by his good looks, his great sense of fashion and style, and his ability to seem relaxed and natural in the glare of public attention. However, it all began with his talent on the soccer field, especially with the goals he scored with his famous bending kicks and the long passes he made to set up goals for others. Had he been an average player, style and looks would not have been enough to keep him in the public eye for so many years.

Adidas's Predator Mania soccer boots are Beckham's shoes of choice.

5

"No Hands, Please"

Many different types of football are played around the world, and in all but one, players use their hands to play the ball. The story is told that this began in England in 1823, when a boy named William Webb Ellis decided to pick up the ball and run with it during a game. He was a student at Rugby School, and this is how the game of rugby football got its name.

The one exception is soccer, which does not allow the use of hands. Doing this is a foul called "hand ball," or "handling." This is why some people say it is the only game that really deserves to be called *foot*ball.

The Rules of the Game

In England during the Middle Ages, games called "mob football" were played by 100 or more players on each side, often with one whole town playing against another. These games were wild, disorganized, and very rough, and many players were badly injured or even killed. Rules were eventually established to control the game and avoid such disasters.

The first known set of rules for soccer was drawn up in the early 1800s at Eton, England's most famous school. The Eton rules resembled the modern game in that the ball had to be moved along by kicking or dribbling, rather than by carrying or

Leading Russian referee Igor Egerov
makes a call in a game in 2007.

throwing it. Also, Eton had a rule against "sneaking" ahead of the ball, from which we get the modern offside rule.

The rules of soccer are called the Laws of the Game, and there are exactly 17 of them. These rules are written by an international group called FIFA (Fedération Internationale de Football Association), which is based in Zurich, Switzerland, and they apply to soccer wherever it is played.

The Eleven

A soccer team is often called an "eleven," because the game is played with eleven players on each side. In soccer, once a player leaves the game he cannot go back in, so a coach has to think carefully before he brings in a substitute player. Even with substitutes, most players will play the whole game, because only three subs are allowed per team.

For many years, substitutes were not allowed at all in soccer. If a player got hurt during a game, he would either have to play on as best he could, or go off the field and leave the team to continue with just ten players. This rule was changed because it was felt that a team might deliberately try to hurt an opposing player so that his team would have to play a man short.

Youth soccer games do not follow the same player rules as professional soccer. Games are often played with only eight players per side, or even fewer such as the popular five-a-side variation. Players are allowed to come back in a game after they go out, and teams are usually allowed to put in as many subs as they want.

Positions on the Field

Soccer does not have strict assigned positions like baseball or American football. The players move all around the field depending on where the ball is and what is going on. However, there are four positions in soccer that each have a certain general responsibility on the field.

The **goalkeeper** is the only player allowed to use his hands, but he can only do this while he is in his own penalty area. The goalkeeper wears a shirt of a unique color so that he will stand out from the other players. A goalkeeper has to be good at stopping and catching the ball, and he is usually tall so that he can reach high shots.

A **defender** plays back near his own goal and his main job is to defend that goal; that is, to keep the other team away and stop them from scoring. A defender must be good at tackling and be able to kick the ball a long way. In professional soccer, a defender also has to be good at heading the ball. A defender is sometimes called a fullback or center-back.

A **midfielder** is so called because he plays in the middle of the field, the area that is not near either goal. Midfielders have to be able to do a lot of running, and they are expected to be good both at passing the ball and at getting it away from the other team.

A **forward** plays close to the other team's goal. A forward is supposed to score goals or set up goals for others. Scoring a goal is the hardest part of professional soccer. Some forwards are tall players who score by heading the ball, while others are small, quick players who can get around a defender.

Systems of Play

A soccer team must have ten outfield players (players other than the goalkeeper), but there is no rule as to how these ten players should be arranged on the field. Most professional teams today use a 4–4–2 system, which means that there are four defenders, four midfielders, and two forwards. Others may use a 3–4–3, 4–3–3, or 4–5–1 system.

In the early days of the game, all teams played with a 2–3–5 system. The players wore numbers according to their position, starting with the goalkeeper as #1. So, if the right defender moved over to play left defender in a certain game, he would change his usual #2 shirt for #3. Fans would know which player was a team's main forward, because he would always be wearing #9.

Teams no longer use the 2–3–5, but the positions on the field are still often numbered that way. For this reason Gary Neville, Manchester United's right defender, wears the #2 shirt that went with this position in the 2–3–5. With many teams it is a special honor to wear the #10 shirt, because many great players of the past have had this number, such as Pelé and Diego Maradona.

Ball In/Out of Play

In soccer, the lines at the edges of the field are part of the playing area. If the ball is on the side of the field and it touches the line, it is still in play. It has to go all the way over the line to be out of play.

The rule for scoring a goal works in the same way. The whole ball has to go all the way over the goal line and into the goal for it to count. If a ball is rolling past the line, and the goalkeeper manages to grab it before it gets all the way over, this is not a goal.

Throw-In

If the ball does go out of play by going all the way over the side-line, then the referee will judge which team was the last to

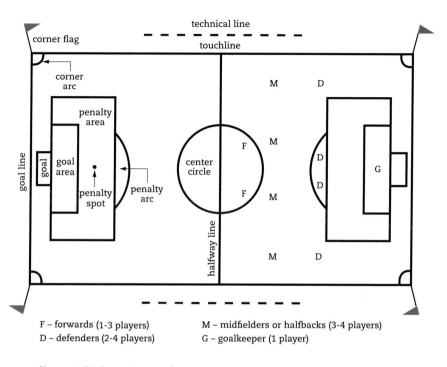

F – forwards (1-3 players)   M – midfielders or halfbacks (3-4 players)
D – defenders (2-4 players)   G – goalkeeper (1 player)

Please note this diagram is not to scale.

touch it before it went out. (The sideline is also called the touch-line for this reason.) Suppose the Reds are playing the Blues, and the Reds put the ball out. The Blues would then get to return the ball to play from outside the field where the ball crossed the sideline by a throw-in. The throw-in is the only time in the game when a player can use his hands to play the ball.

The thrower has to keep both feet on the ground and throw the ball with both hands. He has to stay behind the line, and cannot step out onto the field. If he does not follow these rules, the referee can blow the whistle for an illegal throw-in, and the other team then gets to take the throw-in instead.

Goal Kick

If the ball goes over the goal line (end line) rather than the sideline, it is not returned to play by a throw-in. It is kicked back into play, and the way the kick is taken depends on which team put the ball out.

If the ball goes over the Blues' goal line, and the Reds were the last to touch it, then the Blues get to take a *goal kick* to put the ball back into play. The goal kick has to be taken from a place near the goal, but not in an exact spot. Once the kick is made, no player can touch the ball until it has gone out of the penalty area. If this rule is broken, the kick has to be taken again.

Corner Kick

Suppose the ball goes over the Blues' goal line, and a Blues player was the last to touch it before it went out. The Reds would then get to take a *corner kick* to put the ball back into play. The corner kick is so called because it is taken from the corner of the field, where the goal line meets the sideline.

A corner kick is a good chance for a team to score a goal, because they get to kick the ball right toward the other team's net. The other team has to stand at least 10 yards away until the kick is taken.

A player practices moving with the ball through a series of cones.

Ian Fraser of Canada's national team prepares to take a throw-in.

Major Fouls

The Laws of the Game include various fouls that a referee may call. A player is guilty of a major foul if the referee judges that he has done any of the following in a way that is careless, reckless, or with excessive force:

- kicked or tried to kick an opponent
- tripped or tried to trip an opponent
- jumped at an opponent
- charged an opponent
- struck (hit) or tried to strike an opponent
- pushed an opponent

A player is also guilty of a foul if the referee judges that he has done any of the following four things:

- made contact with the opponent before touching the ball when tackling (See chapter six for a description of tackling.)
- held an opponent
- spat at an opponent
- handled the ball deliberately, except for the goalkeeper within his own penalty area (Note: This "hand ball" rule applies to the arm as well as the hand itself; no part of the hand or arm can be used to play the ball.)

The above list is divided into two parts for a reason. For the four fouls in the second part of the list, the action itself is always a foul. If a player holds an opponent to keep him from getting the ball, the referee does not have to judge how this was done, only that it was done. But for the six fouls in the first part, the referee will judge how the action was done. It may be that a player pushes an opponent, but it is only a light push and not careless, reckless, or excessive. The referee can decide that this push did not interfere with play, and not call a foul.

Law 18

The fact that the referee has some freedom in deciding whether or not to call a foul leads to the idea that the game really has 18 rules, not 17. Law 18 is not written down, but it can be expressed as using "common sense." The referee should not be so strict in applying every single line of the rule book that he causes the game to suffer. Soccer is at its best when play moves along smoothly, without being constantly interrupted by the referee's whistle.

For example, the idea of a throw-in is simply to get the ball back into play. So if a player lifts his foot half an inch from the ground while taking the throw, the referee can let this go even though the rule says it is wrong. It did not really give the player an unfair advantage, and blowing the whistle for this would slow down the game.

A major foul: The F.C. Porto player (wearing blue) has used excessive force while trying to gain possession of the ball.

Free Kick/Penalty Kick

When a team commits one of the fouls listed above, the other team gets to take a *free kick* from the spot where the foul happened. It is "free" because all players on the other team have to move at least 10 yards away from the ball and cannot stop the kicker from taking it. However, the defenders can stand in a line called a "wall" to block the goal.

An area extends 18 yards into the soccer field and 18 yards out to the side of either goal post. This is known as the *penalty area* because if a major foul takes place here it is punished by a special kind of free kick called a *penalty kick*. For a penalty kick, only the goalkeeper and the player taking the kick are allowed to be inside the penalty area. The goalkeeper has to stand on his goal line and cannot move forward until the kick is taken. The kicker is only 12 yards from goal for a penalty kick, so this is a hard shot for the goalkeeper to stop. Studies have shown that about three out of every four times, the kicker will score on a penalty kick.

Penalty kicks are also used in some tournaments when the score is tied at the end of the game. This is called a *penalty shoot-out*. Players from each team take turns with penalty kicks and the team that scores the most wins the game. Sometimes all the players on the team will have to shoot before one team or the other wins.

Indirect Free Kick

In addition to the fouls listed above, there are a number of minor fouls that the referee may call. These include getting in the way of another player who is trying to play the ball, or playing in a dangerous way such as kicking high in the air close to the head of an opposing player.

A minor foul is punished by an *indirect free kick*. It is called "indirect" because unlike the regular (direct) free kick, the ball

Los Angeles Galaxy players set up a wall to block
a free kick in an MLS Cup game.

cannot be kicked directly into the goal. It must be touched by
another player first, or the score does not count.

Offside

A rule that many new fans find hard to understand is *offside*.
Offside means that a player is "off his side" of the field; that is,

Italy's midfielder Alberigo Evani sends a powerful left-footed shot toward Brazil's goalkeeper, Claudio Taffarel, in the 1994 World Cup Final.

ahead of the ball in a way that he should not be. If this happens, he will be called for a foul and the other team will get an indirect free kick.

When the ball is passed to a player in the other team's half of the field, he must have at least two players on the other team who are closer to their goal than he is in order to be onside (not offside). (Usually, but not necessarily, this means the goalkeeper plus one defender.) The idea of the offside rule is that it would be too easy to score if a team could just keep players down by the other goal all the time, waiting for the ball to come to them.

Yellow and Red Cards

A player may commit a foul that is worse than usual, such as engaging in a very rough tackle that sends an opposing player flying, or shouting and cursing at the referee. In such a case the referee will show the player a yellow card. This indicates that he is being given a warning for what he has done. The referee will write the player's name in a small notebook, showing that the player has been "booked."

A player may also commit an especially bad foul, such as punching an opposing player. The referee will then show the red card. The player is "sent off," meaning he must leave the field immediately. His team cannot replace him and they must play with one less player for the rest of the game. A player can also be sent off for getting two yellow cards in the same game.

The system of red and yellow cards was invented by a leading English referee named Ken Aston. There had been great confusion during a game when a player was given a warning by the referee, but did not know this until he read about it in the newspaper the next day because he and the referee spoke different languages. Ken Aston knew that what the game needed was a system for the referee to show what he meant without using words. Aston was driving in his car as he thought about this and he noticed the traffic lights changing from green to yellow to red. The answer came to him: a yellow card for a warning, and a red card for stop (playing).

A referee shows the yellow card to a player who insists he has done nothing wrong.

Following: A referee shows the red card and motions for a player to leave the field immediately.

Fancy Kicks and Other Tricks

A soccer player has to be able to control the ball, pass it to a teammate, send it toward the goal, or get it away from a player on the other team. These actions are called skills. Because of the nature of soccer or football, they all have to be done without the use of hands or arms.

Kicking the Ball

Kicking the ball is the most basic part of the game. In youth soccer, any player who is good at kicking the ball will be an asset, even if he has not yet developed other skills of the game.

Though all professional players are good at kicking, David Beckham stands out among these players. He can send the ball a long way and make it go right where he wants it, either for a shot at a goal or for a pass to a teammate.

Beckham is especially known for the way he can bend the ball when he takes a shot on goal. He does this by hitting the side of the ball at an angle with the front inside of his foot. (As Beckham himself says, he "wraps the foot around the ball.") This makes the ball spin as it goes up into the air, and the spin causes it to curve on the way toward goal.

When a player takes a free kick near the goal, the other team will set up a wall, which is a line of defenders blocking the ball's path to the goal. Being able to "bend it like Beckham" means that you can take the free kick so that the ball goes around the outside of the wall, then curves back to go into the goal.

The Power Kick

The *power kick* is used to send the ball over a long distance. It can be used to take a free kick or goal kick, or in any situation where the idea is to get the ball quickly to another part of the field. If you were to watch a video of Beckham or another professional player using the power kick, you could see that they follow this technique:

- Move toward the ball at a slight angle rather than straight on, with the arms out to the side for balance.
- Put the standing (nonkicking) foot down on the ground near the ball, pointing in the direction the ball should go. The standing foot should be even with the ball, not farther back or forward.
- Keep the head down and over the ball as the kicking foot comes forward. Drive the foot hard into the bottom half of the ball, making contact with the instep—the top part of the foot, where the laces of the soccer shoe are.
- Kick all the way through the ball and let the leg come up afterward, rather than stopping the foot when it hits the ball.

Using Two Feet

The Italian coach Cesare Maldini once said of his more famous son Paolo, "He is a much better player than I was, because he has two feet, while I only had one." Cesare did not literally mean that he had only one foot, but that he was only good at playing the ball with one foot, where his son was good with both. Even at a professional level, only a few players are really "two-footed," with the ability to kick the ball equally well with either foot. Most players are right-footed, so their left foot is the weakest. Coaches will usually try to put a player on the side of the field that allows him to use his stronger foot more often. For this reason a left-footed player will usually play at left back, left midfield, or as a left forward. Most of the time, a player can choose to use his stronger foot to kick the ball, especially when taking a free kick or a corner kick. However, there will be many times in a game when the ball comes to a player on the "wrong" side, and he will not have time to switch it over to the stronger foot. So players have to be able to develop their weaker foot until they can at least play the ball fairly well with that foot, even if they do not really become "two-footed" like Paolo Maldini.

The Overhead Kick

The most difficult skill in soccer, and the most exciting to see when it works, is probably the *overhead kick* for a goal. This occurs when the ball comes to a player when his back is facing

England's Michael Owen makes an overhead kick in a 2005 game against Northern Ireland.

the goal, and he does not have time to control the ball before taking a shot. So he will jump high in the air and kick the ball backward over his head toward the goal. (Defenders may also use the overhead kick to clear the ball away from their own goal.)

It is also called a bicycle kick, because when the kicker strikes the ball, he moves the kicking foot up and the nonkicking foot down at the same time, as if pedaling a bicycle. The great player Pelé was famous for the bicycle kick, and in the soccer movie *Victory* he is shown performing the kick in perfect slow-motion.

Controlling the Ball

It is often said that the most important skill in soccer is the *first touch*. The first touch is the first chance that a player has to control the ball when it comes to him. The better he is at controlling the ball with just this one touch, the better chance he will have to make a play before a defender closes in on him. Ruud van Nistelrooy of Holland is famous for scoring goals, and one of the main reasons he gets so many is his great first touch. He can control the ball in the penalty area and shoot on goal in an instant, even in the midst of a crowd of defenders.

If the ball comes to a player at high speed, or high in the air, or both, he will have to *trap* it in some way in order to control it. To trap means to stop or slow the movement of the ball so that it will be easier to play. The simplest trap is done with the inside of the foot or the ankle, to stop a ball that is rolling along the ground.

If the ball is slightly off the ground, it can be controlled with the *calf trap*, using the inside part of the leg below the knee. A ball that is higher than this would call for a *thigh trap*, using the upper inside part of the leg. A more difficult trap, but one often needed at the professional level, is the *chest trap*, in which a ball dropping from overhead is controlled with the flat surface of the chest, created by leaning backward. A player can also control a high ball with the head, by *heading* it softly down to his feet.

The key to trapping the ball is having a "soft body." This means that as the ball arrives, the player will relax and move the trapping body part slightly backward, in the same direction as the flight of the ball. This cushions the ball as it arrives, allowing it to fall toward the ground close to the player's feet, rather than bouncing off him.

Keeping the Ball Under Control

Once a player has the ball under control, he has to do something with it. One option is to turn with the ball; that is, to move quickly away in a different direction to get free of a defender. Famous players often become known for special turns or moves that they like to use—the Maradona turn, the Rivelino move, the Matthews move, and so on. David Beckham has said that one of his favorites is the Cruyff turn (named for legendary Dutch player Johan Cruyff). For this play, the player sets up as if to pass or shoot straight ahead, but then quickly pushes the ball behind him to the opposite side and moves off in that direction.

Another high-level control skill is *juggling*. To juggle the ball means to keep it up in the air by moving it from one part of the body to another with short, light taps. This can be done from one foot to the other, one leg to the other, the head to the chest, or any combination of these.

Juggling can be used for a few seconds during a game to keep the ball under control while waiting to make a play. It is also one of the best ways to practice ball control, because you have to react quickly and use different parts of the body to keep the ball in the air. When the great player Diego Maradona was a young child, he would go to professional games in Argentina and entertain the crowds at halftime with his amazing skill at juggling the ball.

England's Kelly Smith dribbles the ball toward the goal during a game against the United States in the Women's World Cup of 2007.

Dribbling

To *dribble* means to move the ball along the ground at your feet. It is actually a form of kicking, because the dribble is a series of small, short kicks. A dribble can be used by a defender to move the ball out of danger or by a midfielder to gain enough space to make a pass. Best of all—but also most difficult to do—it can be used by an attacking player to run by defenders and go in for a shot on goal.

Fans love to watch a great dribbler in action, moving down the field past one defender after another as if the ball were attached to his foot. South America is the region best known for producing great dribblers, such as Garrincha and Ronaldinho of Brazil or Diego Maradona and Lionel Messi of Argentina. British fans might argue that some of their players could also rank high in this category, such as George Best, Ryan Giggs, or Jimmy "Jinky" Johnstone. A joke was told of Johnstone that when he got the ball, everyone else on his team could go off for a break, because he would dribble all around the field without losing the ball until they came back.

Passing

Though dribbling is a good way to advance the ball toward the other goal, even the fastest dribblers cannot go as fast as a ball moving through the air or freely along the ground. Also, a dribbler is often at risk of losing the ball to the other team. For these reasons, as well as others, *passing* the ball to other players, rather than dribbling, is the real foundation of the game, especially at the professional level.

The most common pass in the game, and also the simplest to do, is the *push pass*. This is so called because the ball is played with the inside of the foot as the leg moves forward in a pushing movement. The push pass is usually made over a short distance to a teammate who is waiting to receive the ball.

The *long pass* is made with the instep, in a motion similar to the power kick. The idea is to get the ball quickly to a player in a different part of the field; this is also called *switching the play*. The long pass is not as safe as the push pass, since it has a greater chance of being intercepted. But if it can reach a player who is in the open and not covered by a defender, it can lead to an attack on goal.

The *through pass* is played quickly ahead, to try to send the ball through the defenders to a player who is running in behind them. This is a difficult pass to play, but if it works it can provide a good chance to score.

The long pass and the through pass are usually played "early," meaning that the passer will play the ball as soon as he gets it, or even played "first time," meaning that the passer will send the ball away on the first touch. A type of pass that is always played first time is the *wall pass*, or *one-two pass*. This is made between two players who are running near each other. The first player passes to the second and then continues to move forward, and the second player immediately gives him a return pass. It is often used to bypass defenders. The wall pass got its name years ago from street soccer, where boys would pass the ball to themselves by bouncing it off the wall of a nearby building.

The *cross* is a special type of long pass that often leads to a goal. It is made from the side of the field, typically near the corner flag, to a teammate in front of the goal. A cross can be played along the ground, but in the professional game the ball is usually crossed high in the air, so that it will go over the defenders to reach an attacking player.

Making Space

It is often said of soccer that it is "a game of passing and movement." The second part of this, *movement*, is as important as the first. This is also called *making space* or *making yourself available*. You will see this happen all the time when you watch a professional game. For example, if one of the defenders gets the ball near the sideline, the others will immediately make space by moving sideways and slightly backward, so that they are farther away from him and in a better position to get a pass.

A well-executed slide tackle in an international match between Canada (in white) and Jamaica.

The idea of making space is that before a player can make a good pass, another player on his team has to be in a good spot to receive the pass. If all his teammates are just standing still, it will be easy for the other team to cover them and stop a pass from being made. The same applies to the passer himself. As Beckham says, "Never admire your pass." This means that after the passer has played the ball, he should not stand watching it, but should move into space to be ready for a return pass.

Heading

After the foot, the part of the body most often used to move the ball is the head. The ball is often in the air above the players' heads, and much of the time it is better to strike it with the head than to bring it down to the feet. This is especially true when a high ball is near the goal. Players on the attacking team will try to *head* the ball into the goal, and defenders will try to head it away.

Professional players have many different ways of heading the ball. They may use the side of the head to move the ball quickly to a nearby teammate, or they may use the top of the head to send the ball farther along in the same direction it is already going. The most common type of header is done with the forehead, because its hard, flat surface gives the player the best chance to get power on the ball. It is exciting to see a player race into the penalty area just at the moment that a long pass is arriving and jump up to head the ball into the goal.

Beckham heads the ball while under strong pressure from an opposing player.

Tackling

The act of getting the ball away from a player on the other team is called a *tackle*. In this case the word *tackle* means "to try to take away the ball with the foot or leg" and not "to grab and hold a player with the arms," as the term is used in American football. The most common form of tackle takes place when a player is dribbling the ball up the field and a defender moves in front of him and puts in a foot to knock the ball away.

It is said that there is really only one team playing soccer in a game, the one with the ball. The other team is chasing them, trying to get the ball, so that they can play. A team may have players with the talent to score goals, but someone else on the team has to do the hard work of tackling, or else this talent can't be used.

In an international match between Sweden and Russia, a Swedish forward flies through the air after contact with a Russian defender.

A player might also be an effective defender without having to tackle to take the ball away. He may sense where a pass is going and move in to intercept it. He can get in the way of a player's path to goal, making the player stop and pass to someone else, or he can move in quickly on a player about to receive the ball, so that the player feels pressured and fails to control it.

Marking

The defending player who is closest to the opposing player with the ball will usually try to get it away from him, but, in addition to this, the other players on the team should *mark* the opposing players who do not have the ball. To mark, or cover, a player means to stay near him to stop him from getting the ball, or to block the player's move if he does get it. The nearer to the goal the ball is, the more important it is to have tight marking.

Marking is based on the idea of "Goalside, Inside." *Goalside* means the marker should always be closer to his own goal than the player that he is defending it from, and *inside* means he should be closer to the middle of the field than that player.

Fair Play

Playing the game in a fair way has been an important principle since the beginning of the sport. The best team in the early years of the game was an English club called the Corinthians. (A famous team in Brazil still uses this name in honor of them.) They became known for the Corinthian spirit, which meant playing in a fair, proper way. If the Corinthians were attacking the goal and noticed that an opposing player was hurt, they would stop the game to help him, thinking it would not be right to try to score while a player was down. This tradition still exists in the game today. If a player is hurt and the other team has the ball, they are expected to kick it out of bounds on purpose, so that the injured player can be taken care of. Fans will boo a team if they do not do this.

In important tournaments such as the World Cup, a Fair Play award is given to the team that best follows the rules and plays the game in the right way. Brazil is the team that has won the most World Cups, and also the team that has won the most World Cup Fair Play awards. Winning and good sportsmanship do go together.

Unfortunately, there are some players who think that the best way to win is to break the rules, or at least to bend them a little. An example of this in the current game is diving. To dive means to fall to the ground in a dramatic, exaggerated way, so that the referee will think there has been a foul. Players are more likely to do this when they have been bumped or touched in the penalty area, hoping to get a penalty kick. Fans do not like to see

Soccer is a sport of constant
motion. A player must be fit to
use his skills most effectively.

a player dive. They will often make fun of the player who dives by holding up scorecards with "10" on them, as if he were an Olympic diver getting a perfect score. They will even give an "Oscar" award for Best Actor, to the player who pretends he has been fouled or hurt most often.

Fitness

Though it is not a skill, fitness is just as important to a player as his soccer abilities. Being fit means to be in good physical condition, free from injury, and able to play at one's best. Without fitness, a player cannot use his skills.

Though professional athletes in all sports have to be very fit, this is especially true of soccer players, since the game involves so much running. A game lasts for 90 minutes, and the clock continues to run for the entire time, with no time-outs, except for the halftime break. It has been estimated that the average player will run about 5–6 miles in a typical professional game. (That does not include the goalkeeper, and goalkeepers typically are able to play to an older age because they do not have to do as much running.)

In soccer, players do not wear as much protective equipment as in other sports such as hockey or American football, because the game does not involve as much heavy physical contact. The uniform for the game consists only of shirt, shorts, socks, and shoes, and the only protective item allowed is a pair of shin guards, which are worn under the socks. Soccer is a relatively safe sport in spite of this lack of protection—or perhaps because of it—since players do not charge into each other as they might if they were heavily padded.

Players compete to win the ball in a one-on-one practice drill.

7

Women and Girls on the Field

The game of soccer is no longer played just by men. A world-wide study by FIFA, the governing body of soccer, shows that 26 million women and girls now play soccer around the globe. Since the previous survey of this kind six years earlier, the number of females playing regularly on an official team has more than doubled, and the number of female youth players has increased by one third.

Soccer for women and girls is especially popular in North America; almost one out of every three female players in the world lives in the U.S. or Canada. In the U.S., about 40% of all soccer players are female, and in Canada the figure is 33%. These two countries also have strong women's national teams, both of which finished in the top four at the 2003 Women's World Cup.

Women's World Cup

The FIFA Women's World Cup was first held in 1991 in China and is played on a four-year cycle like the Men's World Cup. The United States won in 1991 and then again in 1999. The other three Cups have been won by Norway (1995) and Germany (2003, 2007).

Women's soccer is also a sport in the Olympics. The first women's soccer competition in the Olympics was held in 1996

Swedish players congratulate Hanna Ljungberg
(#10) for her goal against Germany in the
Women's World Cup Final of 2003.

in Atlanta, Georgia, and the U.S. Women's team won the gold medal. Shannon MacMillan scored game-winning goals for the U.S. against Sweden and Norway, and another against China in the final.

The U.S.-China game was played in front of more than 76,000 people, the largest number of fans ever to watch a women's sports event until that time. The size of this crowd, and the extensive coverage given to the U.S. team on television and in the press, made many people aware of women's soccer for the first time.

U.S. goalkeeper Briana Scurry dives to block a penalty kick in the Women's World Cup Final of 1999.

The Olympics in 1996 was the first big step for women's soccer in America, but the event that really put it in the spotlight was the Women's World Cup of 1999. As in the Olympics, the U.S. faced China in the final, which was held at the huge Rose Bowl stadium in Pasadena, California.

More than 90,000 fans were at the Rose Bowl that day to see one of the most famous games in U.S. soccer history. The crowd included President Bill Clinton, a fan of the sport from the time his daughter, Chelsea, played for her school. The U.S. and China played the regular 90-minute game without a goal being scored, and neither team managed to score during 30 minutes of extra time. The Cup winner would have to be decided by penalty kicks.

In a penalty shoot-out the winning team is the one with the most goals after five penalty shots each. The first four U.S.

players successfully scored, as did their Chinese counter-parts. It all came down to the fifth shooter, defender Brandi Chastain. U.S. goalkeeper Briana Scurry had stopped one shot from China, so a goal by Chastain would give the United States the win at 5–4.

A Worldwide Celebration

Brandi Chastain put her penalty kick right into the goal and so began a huge celebration. Chastain herself set this off as she pulled off her uniform shirt, waved it overhead, and then dropped to her knees on the field, shaking her fists with joy.

Although it is common in men's soccer for a player to take off his shirt to celebrate scoring a goal, people had not seen a female player do this before. A photo taken at that moment shows Chastain in white uniform shorts and a dark blue sports bra, holding her uniform shirt in one hand. The photo was seen in newspapers everywhere and often appeared on television and on the Internet. *Newsweek* magazine had it on their cover with the headline "Girls Rule!" (This was an interesting choice of words since Chastain, the "girl" pictured, was almost 31 years old at the time). The image became so famous that when Chastain wrote a book about soccer, its title was *It's Not About the Bra.*

Brandi Chastain whips off her jersey to celebrate her successful penalty kick.

"Mia, Mia, Mia!"

Following its World Cup victory, the U.S. women's national team had a level of fame and status that the men's team had never achieved. At that time the men's team practiced at an Olympic training center in Southern California. Several dozen fans might show up for a game, and they would be allowed to stand right along the sidelines with the team. Any fan could strike up a conversation with coach Bruce Arena or with one of the players.

When the women's team came to play at the same location, hundreds, not dozens, of people showed up to surround the field and watch the team, carrying signs and banners for their favorite players. No longer could fans roam the sidelines as with the men's team. Security guards were everywhere and fences separated the players and the fans. Young girls dressed in the uniforms of their own youth soccer teams shouted "Mia, Mia!" to cheer for the team's leading scorer, Mia Hamm.

The U.S. World Cup team had stars at every position, with Briana Scurry in goal, and Joy Fawcett, Brandi Chastain, Carla Overbeck, and Kate Sobrero on defense. The midfielders were Michelle Akers, voted the world's greatest female player of all time, and two other great U.S. players, Kristine Lilly and Julie Foudy. The forwards were Hamm, playing in a free role, and Tiffeny Milbrett and Cindy Parlow providing a small-player/big-player combination up front. Shannon MacMillan was the "super-sub," coming off the bench to give the team a lift when needed.

These players were popular not only for their soccer talent, but for how they presented themselves. They were not as involved in off-field problems as some professional male athletes had been, and they were focused on team play, not on getting attention as individuals. Hamm, the team's most famous player, was so modest that whenever an interviewer started to talk about her personal goal scoring records, she would change the subject to what a good job her teammates were doing.

A defender's nightmare: Mia Hamm
closes in for an attack on goal.

A League of Their Own

It seemed that with this kind of support it was time to start a professional league for women in the United States. WUSA (Women's United Soccer Association) was founded in 2001 with eight teams around the U.S. The top American players were assigned to different teams based on some connection with the area. For example, Brandi Chastain played in the city where she was born, San Jose, California; New England native Kristine Lilly joined the Boston team, and Shannon MacMillan was with the

Joy Fawcett (left) and Cindy Parlow celebrate the United States' victory in the 1996 Women's Soccer Olympics.

Spirit in her home county of San Diego. Many star players from other countries also came to America to play in WUSA, such as Birgit Prinz of Germany, Dagny Mellgren of Denmark, Charmaine Hooper of Canada, Sissi of Brazil, and Sun Wen of China.

The excitement of World Cup 1999 carried over to WUSA and the league got off to a good start in terms of game attendance, drawing average crowds of about 8,300 per match. However, the

TV audience was smaller than had been expected, and few large companies wanted to sponsor the league. There was also a warning sign in the fact that a lot of the fans focused their attention on just two players: Mia Hamm and Brandi Chastain. Chastain was a good player but, frankly, not the league's best, and her appeal was based mainly on her famous "shirtless" celebration.

WUSA had an original bank account of $40 million, which was supposed to last for five years; however, the league spent all the money in the first year of play. WUSA did continue for two more seasons after this, but then went out of business in 2003. Today, some U.S. women play in the W-League or in foreign professional leagues, but the main opportunity for the top players is now the national team, just as it was in the days before WUSA. In 2007, a group called the Women's Soccer Initiative (WSI) announced a plan to bring women's professional soccer back to the U.S., with an eight-team league scheduled to start play in 2009.

College Soccer for Women

Although there is currently no top professional women's league in America, female soccer players do have a great opportunity to play college soccer. Universities such as North Carolina, UCLA, Portland, and Notre Dame have women's teams that win championships, produce players for the national team, and play before enthusiastic crowds.

College soccer does not just attract American players. The film *Bend It Like Beckham* tells the story of two girls who dream of being successful soccer players. Their dream is not to join a soccer club in England, as would be the case for boys their age (and as it was for Beckham himself), but to go to the United States to play college soccer for Santa Clara University in California. The characters think of American college soccer as the best opportunity that a female player can have. In a real-life version of this story, English player Kelly Smith came to the United States to play for Seton Hall University of New Jersey in the late 1990s, and she became the leading scorer in all of college soccer.

8

Soccer Schools and Scholarships

Soccer is a popular sport with young people all around the world. It is easy to play, it does not involve expensive equipment, and it doesn't require a special place for a game, just enough room to kick around a ball. The president of the South American country Bolivia recently organized a game that took place on a snow-covered mountain 20,000 feet high, to show that soccer can be played anywhere.

Youth Soccer in America

In North America, young people usually play in a soccer club. These clubs play either recreational (rec) soccer or competitive soccer. In recreational programs such as AYSO (American Youth Soccer Organization), all players who sign up to play are placed on a team. In competitive soccer, players have to be invited to play, and there may be more players trying out for a club than there are places available.

Competitive teams are often called "traveling teams," because they go to other towns to play against each other, while a rec team usually plays against other teams within the same town.

Usually only children who live in a town can play in its recreational league, but a competitive team can have players

Young people around the world like to play soccer, including this novice Buddhist monk in Laos.

Evo Morales, the president of Bolivia, shows off his soccer
skills on top of a mountain, 20,000 feet above sea level.

from anywhere. Clint Dempsey, now a member of the U.S. national team and a professional player in England, played for a team in Dallas, Texas, that was a three-hour drive from his home.

Soccer Academies

In Europe, youth soccer is played in local clubs as in America, but the best players are not part of this system. They play for the youth teams of professional clubs such as Ajax (Holland), AC Milan (Italy), or Barcelona (Spain). These youth teams are also known as "academies," and the idea is that players are taught how to play the game, like students in a school. The hope is that the best of these young players will go on to play for the professional team. For example, the Liverpool Academy has produced a number of players who became stars for Liverpool F.C., including Robbie Fowler, Michael Owen, Steven Gerrard, and Jamie Carragher. It's reported that Gerrard, the team's current captain, was first noticed by Liverpool scouts when he was only eight years old.

The David Beckham Academy is a recent development in youth soccer. Beckham has often said how much he learned as a boy at the Bobby Charlton Soccer School, and he wanted to give other children the same chance that he had. The Academy offers summer camps for boys and girls of all ability levels, aged 8 to 15. The camp program was set up by Beckham's friend Eric Harrison, who was his youth team coach at Manchester United. There, Harrison trained not only Beckham, but other future stars such as Ryan Giggs, Paul Scholes, and Gary Neville. So the campers will be performing the same drills that Beckham and the others did as youth players. At present, the Beckham Academy has two locations, one in London and the other in Los Angeles. Future openings are planned for sites in Asia.

The United States Soccer Federation (USSF) sponsors an academy in Bradenton, Florida, whose goal is to select and train the 40 best young American players. Players who join the Bradenton Academy become part of a full-time program in which they live right at the training facility and practice and play soccer almost every day. Some of the top current U.S. players were part of the Bradenton program, such as Landon Donovan, DaMarcus Beasley, and Eddie Johnson.

In 2007, the USSF began the Soccer Development Academy. A number of youth soccer teams across the country, 64 in all, have been invited to join the academy. These include such leading clubs as F.C. Delco of Philadelphia, Chicago Magic, Solar F.C. of Texas, Nomads of San

Beckham watches as players practice soccer skills at the David Beckham Academy in Greenwich, England.

Below: Beckham poses with young players at the American branch of his Soccer Academy near Los Angeles, California.

Diego, and Real SoCal (the team that David Beckham's son Brooklyn joined when the family moved to Los Angeles). It is hoped that this new academy will encourage the development of players in the same fashion as the leading professional clubs of Europe and South America. The long-term goal is to find players who can play for the U.S. national team in the future. At present, most of the players on the national team did not develop through the Bradenton Academy or through other all-star youth teams. Instead, they were first noticed during their college career, or while playing minor league soccer.

Many American soccer fans feel that the country's current youth game puts too much value on a strong, physical player, and not enough on ball skills. David Beckham was small for his age as a boy, and as a result he did not always get to play for his youth team. Even today, he is not the biggest or the strongest player on the field. But his ball skills set him apart from other players—skills like hitting a 60-yard pass so that it gently drops down in an exact spot, or stopping the ball dead when it comes to him, no matter how fast it is going.

Soccer Scholarships

In Europe there are hundreds of professional teams, which means that there are a lot of opportunities for young players within these teams. Major League Soccer has only 13 teams, so opportunities for young players are much more limited. For this reason, youth soccer clubs try to develop players mainly to play college soccer as opposed to professional soccer. At the present time, about 400 colleges in the U.S. and Canada offer scholarships for men's soccer players, and more than 500 for women's soccer.

The large number of colleges offering soccer scholarships does not mean that all the players on the team will have scholarships. The National Collegiate Athletic Association, the ruling group of American college sports, limits soccer teams to 9 scholarships for men and 12 for women. The typical team will have more than 20 players, so there are not enough scholarships for all team members. Also, the coach will divide the scholarship money that is available among different players, so that only a few star players actually get full scholarships. However, playing soccer might help someone get into a top college, because a certain number of places in each freshman class will be set aside for student-athletes.

From the Streets to Greatness

An important question about youth soccer is whether social conditions help to develop the best players. The great players of the past in South America and Europe tended to grow up in crowded city neighborhoods, where there were lots of other boys around to get a soccer game going. They would play every day in a nearby park or field, or even in the street when no grass was available. The other players might be their own age, or they might be older or younger, depending on who turns up to play that day. The game could last a few minutes or go on almost all day. Most important, there would be no coaches telling the boys what to do. They would have to decide on their own what kind of play to make.

Later on, these great players did join organized teams and get coaching from professionals. But many experts argue that it was from playing street soccer, not club soccer, that players such as Pelé, Diego Maradona, George Best, Johan Cruyff, or Zinedine Zidane developed their great skill with the ball, and their a bility to see the whole field and make unexpected plays. Because of this, legendary Dutch coach Rinus Michels, who was voted the greatest coach of the 20th century, says "street soccer is the most natural educational system that can be found."

9

Greats of the Game

The following individuals have been important to the game of soccer. This is not a list of the greatest players of all time, though many of the names here would be on that list. These are people who have left their mark on the sport.

Roman Abramovich Russian oil billionaire and the owner of England's Chelsea club. He bought the team in 2003 and soon became famous for the amount of money he spent on it. He poured hundreds of millions of dollars into buying star players from other teams, and, under his ownership, Chelsea won the FA Premier in 2005 and 2006.

Freddy Adu U.S. player, born in Ghana. He made history as the youngest professional athlete in U.S. sports history when he signed with D.C. United of Major League Soccer (MLS) at the age of 14, and again in 2006 when he became the youngest player ever to play for the U.S. national team. In July 2007 he left MLS to join Benfica, a famous club of Portugal.

Michelle Akers U.S. player voted the best female player ever in an official world poll. She played 15 years for the U.S. national team and led them to two Women's World Cup championships and an Olympic gold medal.

Pelé, during his career with the New York Cosmos.

Roberto Baggio Italian player noted for ball skills and tricky moves. Known as Il Codino Divino (the Divine Ponytail) for his favorite hairstyle and his stylish way of playing.

Gordon Banks English goalkeeper who helped England win the 1966 World Cup. He later competed in the North American Soccer League. He made a famous diving save against Pelé in the 1970 World Cup that many call the greatest save of all time.

Franz Beckenbauer German player rated as the greatest defender ever to play the game. He was known as Der Kaiser (the Emperor) for the way he could rule over a game from his sweeper position. Beckenbauer was one of only two people to win the Cup both as player and coach. He played for the great New York Cosmos team of the North American Soccer League, a team that also featured Pelé.

David Beckham English midfield player and currently the most famous player of the game.

George Best Attacking player for Manchester United and Northern Ireland, and considered the most talented player ever produced in the British Isles. He was the first soccer player to have "pop star" celebrity status. He wore a Beatles-style haircut, and was at the height of his game in the 1960s, when the Beatles were at the top of the music scene.

Jean Marc Bosman A Belgian who became one of the most influential players in the history of the sport by winning a court case to end rules dictating which team a player could join. The result (the "Bosman Rule") gave greater freedom to players

Clockwise from top left: Gordon Banks of England, the Irish genius George Best, "Der Kaiser" Franz Beckenbauer of Germany, and Italy's Roberto Baggio.

to move to different teams, especially foreign teams. Now, clubs such as Arsenal or Chelsea in the English Premier League can field an entire team of foreign players.

Matt Busby Scottish player and coach, manager of Manchester United from 1945–1969, during which time the team won the European Cup, two FA Cups, and five league titles. He produced a generation of young, exciting players known as the "Busby Babes."

Eric Cantona French forward who came to Manchester United in the early 1990s, when the club had not won the Football League for 26 years. He immediately led them to the championship with his ability to score goals and set them up for others. In a period of eight years, United won the League six times with Cantona, and the only time they did not win was when he was suspended for attacking a fan who had been shouting insults at him.

Antonio Carbajal Mexican goalkeeper who was the first player to appear in five different World Cup tournaments, representing his country in the competitions of 1950, '54, '58, '62, and '66.

Alberto Carlos Outstanding defender who was captain of Brazil's 1970 World Cup championship team, which was voted best team of all time. Provided great support for Pelé with Brazil, with their club team Santos, and then with the New York Cosmos.

John Charles Welsh player famous both as a goal scoring forward and a defender. He was a star in England for Leeds United, and for Juventus in Italy, where they nicknamed him Il Buon Gigante, "the Gentle Giant." He was said to have been such a sportsmanlike player that he was never once cautioned by the referee during his career.

Bobby Charlton One of the world's best-known and most popular players. Often rated as the player who has meant the most to Manchester United in the team's history. He led the

English national team to the World Cup title in 1966, and he still holds the record for the most goals scored for England. His brother, Jack Charlton, was also part of the 1966 World Cup team.

Brandi Chastain A member of the U.S. team that won the 1999 Women's World Cup. When she scored the game-winning goal in a penalty kick shootout, she gained instant fame both for the goal itself and for removing her shirt and waving it in the air in celebration.

Pierluigi Collina Italian referee, generally regarded as the best referee of the modern era. He was known for his ability to let a game flow smoothly while still keeping control of the action. Easy to recognize because of his completely bald head and the powerful stare he would direct at the (rare) player who questioned his decisions.

Johan Cruyff (also spelled Cruijff) Dutch player who was named in an official poll as the best European player of the 20th century. He was the leader of the teams that established the idea of "Total Football" in the early 1970s. When he went to play for Barcelona of Spain he was called El Salvador (The Savior), because he was thought to have rescued the team.

Kenny Dalglish Scottish player known as "King Kenny" to fans of Liverpool F.C. and voted by them as the team's top player of all time. As player and manager, he won the largest collection of honors of any individual, including 3 European Cups, 13 League championships (9 English, 4 Scottish), and 10 domestic cups (5 English and 5 Scottish).

Rick Davis U.S. midfield player who was part of the New York Cosmos team of Pelé and Beckenbauer. Noted as the first outstanding American player to be developed under the modern U.S. system of youth soccer.

William (Dixie) Dean The greatest goal scorer in the history of the English game, especially famous for his ability to head the ball. He had a reported 379 goals in 438 games and also holds the record for one season with 60 goals in 39 games in the 1927–28 league season for Everton F.C.

Alfredo Di Stefano Argentina-born forward famous for his play with Real Madrid of Spain. The team was champion of Europe five times in a row during his years there. He ranks with Pelé, Diego Maradona, and Johan Cruyff on the short list for greatest player of all time. Played top-level soccer until the age of nearly 40 and reportedly scored close to 900 goals.

Didi Brazilian player famous for his "falling leaf" kick, so called because the ball would flutter and dip through the air like a leaf falling from a tree.

Landon Donovan U.S. forward/midfielder generally considered the most talented current U.S. player. A teammate of David Beckham's with the Los Angeles Galaxy.

Eusebio Portugal's greatest player and one of the best of all time in Europe. He was born in Africa and he is known as the player who began the movement of outstanding African players to teams in Europe.

Alex Ferguson The most successful manager of the modern British game. He became "Sir Alex" for his great achievements at Manchester United, especially for winning the European Cup, FA Cup, and English Premier League all in the same season.

Garrincha Brazilian player famous for his brilliant dribbling and dangerous free kicks, nicknamed "The Little Bird." He was crippled as a child and had to have an operation to walk properly, then went on to become one of the fastest runners in soccer.

Landon Donovan

Paul Gascoigne Creative, highly skilled midfield player for England, nicknamed "Gazza." He was one of the stars of the 1990 World Cup, the most enduring image of which is that of Gazza crying on receipt of a yellow card that would have kept him from the final.

Ryan Giggs Welsh player who has had a great career at Manchester United. He has played over 500 games for United to date and holds the team record for most trophies won. Known for his great speed and the ability to take the ball past defenders down the left sideline, he is often named by fans of other teams as the United player they most wish their team had.

Paul "Gazza" Gascoigne

Ruud Gullit Dutch player known for his fluid playing style and distinctive "dreadlocks" hair. He was said to have been the ideal player for the Dutch game of Total Football because of his great all-around ability.

Mia Hamm U.S. female player considered the single person most responsible for the interest in women's and girl's soccer in America. She is currently the leading goal scorer of all time in the international women's game.

Owen Hargreaves Canadian midfield player with Manchester. He could have played international soccer for Canada, for any of the nations of the British Isles based on his family background, or even for Germany based on having lived there. He finally chose England and is a key player in their current team.

Glenn Hoddle A talented midfield player noted especially for ball control and long passing ability. An all-time great for Tottenham Hotspur and also celebrated in France for his later career at Monaco.

Geoff Hurst English forward who scored three goals in the 1966 World Cup Final to lead England to victory, becoming the only player to date to record a three-goal "hat trick" in the Final.

Alex James Scottish player for the famous Arsenal teams of the 1930s, known for the long, baggy uniform shorts he wore. He is considered to have invented the position of attacking midfielder, an important part of the modern game.

Elton John Famous British pop singer (born Reginald Dwight) known for his lifelong devotion to the Watford Football Club. At various times he has served as owner and chairman of the Watford club and he still holds the title of honorary president.

Vinnie Jones Colorful and controversial player for various English clubs, most notably Wimbledon when they were known as the "Crazy Gang." Notorious for violent incidents both on and off the field and reportedly shown the red card 13 different times in his career. Later appeared in movies such as *Lock, Stock and Two Smoking Barrels*; *Gone in Sixty Seconds*; and *Mean Machine*; in which he played "hard man" characters of the same type as his soccer image.

Mario Kempes High-scoring Argentinian forward, nicknamed El Matador (The Bullfighter). Star of the 1978 World Cup in which he scored six goals, including two in his team's final game victory against Holland.

Jurgen Klinsmann The leading forward for the German national team during its period of great success in the 1990s, noted for his great speed. Made over 100 appearances in all for Germany and recorded more than 50 goals, including 11 in the World Cup. Also coached Germany successfully in the 2006 World Cup. He currently lives in the U.S., where it is rumored that he will take up a coaching position.

Denis Law Scottish forward noted for spectacular goals, especially through the use of the overhead (bicycle) kick. A star for Manchester United, he also scored 30 goals in 55 matches for Scotland.

Kristine Lilly Left-footed player for the U.S. women's national team, part of the "golden generation" of players who won the Women's World Cup and the Olympic Games. The first player in soccer history, male or female, to play 200 times for the national team and has since gone on to make well over 300 appearances.

Gary Lineker English player rated as the country's leading forward of the 1980s and early 90s. Top scorer in the 1986 World Cup and also a star in the 1990 tournament. Had a role in the film *Bend It Like Beckham* along with two other famous former players, Alan Hansen and John Barnes.

Diego Maradona

Paolo Maldini Italian defender who is often named in polls as the best left back ever to play the game. Has played more games than any other player for the Italian national team. He first played for the leading Italian club AC Milan at the age of 16, and as of this writing he is still with the team at age 39 and still one of the top defenders in the world.

Diego Maradona Argentina's best player, and voted in one recent poll as the world's greatest ever, above even Pelé. He played in three World Cups and led his team to victory in 1986. In one Cup game that year, he scored what has been voted the greatest goal of all time when he ran with the ball past half the other team before scoring. In the same game, he also scored what has been called the worst goal in Cup history, when he illegally knocked the ball into the goal with his hand. Asked about this afterward, he said the goal was scored not by his hand but by "the Hand of God."

Lothar Matthäus German midfielder/defender who is one of only two players to date to have played in five World Cups. He also held the world record for most international games played, eventually retiring after playing 150.

Stanley Matthews English player who had the longest career of any player at the top level from the 1930s through the 60s. Began in the Football League at the age of 17 and continued to play there until he was past 50. He would line up along the right sideline and he was known for his great ability to take the ball past defenders.

Rinus Michels Dutch coach credited with pioneering the idea of Total Football, a stylish, entertaining type of play, which stresses all-around skills. He was voted the top coach of the 20th century in an official poll.

Roger Milla Cameroon forward known as the "Ageless Wonder" of African soccer. He set a record by playing in the 1994 World Cup at the age of 42.

Bobby Moore Captain of the 1966 England team that won the World Cup and also an important member of the 1962 and 1970 teams. Named by Pelé as the best defender he ever played against, and is often placed alongside Franz Beckenbauer in defense on all-time all-star teams.

Gerd Müller German forward, nicknamed "Der Bomber." Often rated as the best pure goal scorer of all time for his great scoring record with West Germany and with his club team Bayern Munich.

Daniel Passarella Outstanding defender for Argentina and captain of the 1978 team that won the World Cup. Famous especially for scoring a record number of goals for a defender through his ability to head the ball.

Pelé Brazilian forward of the 1950s to 1970s, the world's most famous soccer player and generally thought to be the greatest ever. He had a complete range of skills but was known in particular for the ability to control and play any ball that came to him. He joined the Brazilian national team at age 17 and won three of the four World Cups in which he played. He then joined the New York Cosmos and almost single-handedly made Americans aware of the sport of soccer. Pelé is so respected around the world that he once stopped a war in Africa because all the people who were fighting wanted to see him play.

Frantisek Planicka Czechoslovakia's star goalkeeper of the 1930s and one of the sports heroes of his country. He is famous for a playing in a brutal World Cup game in 1938 against Brazil (called "the Battle of Bordeaux"), in which he suffered a broken arm yet managed to finish the match.

Michel Platini French midfielder considered the best player from his country prior to Zinedine Zidane, and a regular choice in midfield for all-time European and World teams. He was the first player ever to be named European Player of the Year three years in a row.

Vittorio Pozzo Legendary manager of the Italian national team from 1929 to 1948, the only manager to win two World Cups in a row. Also managed the Italian Olympic champions in 1936. His association with Italian dictator Benito Mussolini made him a controversial figure.

Ferenc Puskas Hungarian forward known especially for his great left-footed shot. Undefeated for four years, he led the Hungary team of the early 1950s which brought a new style of play to the game. He left Hungary to escape Communist rule and became a star at Real Madrid when they had the best club team in Europe.

Alf Ramsey English manager who led the national team to the World Cup championship in 1966. One of the few people to have won the Football League as both a player and a manager.

Romario Brazilian forward who is described as the best goal scorer of the current era. He claims to have scored more than 1,000 goals in his career, which would be second only to Pelé (but this number is questioned).

Ronaldinho Artistic player who provides the best current example of how "the beautiful game" is played by the national team of Brazil. Also has had great success with his club, Barcelona. Very popular with fans because of the joy and enthusiasm he brings to the game.

Ronaldo Brazilian player combining speed, power, and skill, to score many important goals for his country. He was expected to be the leading player in the World Cup of 1998, but he played poorly in its final and Brazil lost. He then made a comeback in the 2002 World Cup, leading his team to victory as the top scorer.

Cristiano Ronaldo Portuguese player noted for great dribbling ability. Playing for Manchester United in 2006–07, he became the first person to win Player of the Year, Young Player of the Year, and Fans' Player of the Year all in the same season. Said to have been named for his father's favorite actor, Ronald Reagan.

Wayne Rooney Forward for Manchester United, often described as the best young English player since the late Duncan Edwards. He joined Everton F.C. at age 16, and became the youngest player ever to score a League goal. He also became the youngest player ever to appear for the England national team and to score a goal for them.

Hugo Sanchez High-scoring forward of the 1980s and 90s, generally regarded as Mexico's greatest player ever. Became well-known for his enthusiastic celebrations after scoring a goal, highlighted by a complete somersault in the air.

Peter Schmeichel Danish goalkeeper, a huge man known for the way he commanded his team's defense and for his shot-stopping ability. Goalkeeper for Manchester United when they dominated the English game in the 1990s.

Bill Shankly Scottish manager and player who was very successful as the head of Liverpool F.C. Known for saying "Some people think football is a matter of life and death. They are wrong. It is much more important than that."

Alan Shearer English forward, the top goal scorer to date in the history of the English Premier League, especially for Newcastle United in the city of his birth. Also played over 60 games for England with 30 goals scored.

Matthias Sindelar Austrian forward, the leader of the famous Wonder Team that played the best soccer in Europe in the 1930s. He was nicknamed "The Paper Man" because of his thin, pale appearance. He died mysteriously in 1939, shortly after Nazi Germany took over his home country of Austria. It has been rumored that this led him to commit suicide or that he was murdered by the Nazis.

Sylvester Stallone Not a soccer player, but the star of a famous soccer movie, *Victory* (1981). The movie is set in a World War II German prison camp, and Stallone plays an American who has never played soccer before, but is called upon to be the goalkeeper in a game between the prisoners and a German military team.

Rod Stewart Scottish pop singer known for his love of soccer. He is a strong supporter of both the Scotland national team and the famous Celtic F.C. team of Glasgow, Scotland. Also a good player himself, he has often appeared in celebrity games as well as playing in an amateur league in Los Angeles.

Carlos Valderrama "El Pibe," a midfield player for Colombia known for his great ability to pass the ball and for his distinctive bushy hairstyle. Colombian fans would often show up at a game wearing their hair in the same style.

George Weah Liberian forward who was chosen as the best African player of the 20th century. He won championships in both France and Italy and was the leading scorer of the 1995 European Cup.

Charles Wreford-Brown A star player for Oxford University in the late 1800s who is given credit for inventing the word "soccer." It is said that a friend asked him if he planned to go play "rugger," or rugby football, and he answered, "No, I'm going to play 'soccer.'"

Lev Yashin Russian goalkeeper who is often rated as the greatest of all time at the position. He played in three different World Cups and is the only goalkeeper to win the European Player of the Year award. He founded the modern approach to goalkeeping, in which a keeper is expected to cover the whole penalty area rather than waiting in the goal for a shot to be taken.

Zico Brazilian player often rated as second only to Pelé among players to wear the famous number 10 shirt for his country. Star of the 1982 Brazil team that is called the best team not to reach the World Cup Final.

Zinedine Zidane French midfielder (of Algerian parents) considered to be the best all-around player of the current era. Led France to the 1998 World Cup championship and won both European Player of the Year and World Player of the Year honors. His career came to an unfortunate end in 2006 when he was sent off in the World Cup Final for head-butting an opponent.

Zinedine "Zizou" Zidane

index

A page reference in **bold** indicates an illustration.

A

Abramovich, Roman, 123
AC Milan, 117, 134
Adams, Tony, 55, 59
Adams, Victoria. See Beckham, Victoria
Adidas, 7, 64
Adu, Freddy, 17, 123
AEG, 11
agents, 8
Ajax, 117
Akers, Michelle, 110, 123
American Idol, 8
American Youth Soccer Organization (AYSO), 115
Arena, Bruce, 110
Argentina, 12, 27, 44, 54
Arsenal F.C., 10, 17, 56, 57, 131
Aston, Ken, 82
attendance figures in North America, 12, 15, 17

B

Baggio, Roberto, 124, **125**
ball in/out of play, 70
Banks, Gordon, 124, **125**
Barraza, Rene, 23–24
Barcelona (soccer team), 48, 117, 127, 136
Barnes, John, 132
baseball, 11, 12
basketball, 11, 12
Bayern Munich, 55, 135
Beasley, DaMarcus, 119
Beckenbauer, Franz, 124, **125**, 127, 135
Beckham, Brooklyn, 8, 62, 120
Beckham, Cruz, 8, 62
Beckham, David, **6**, 7–8, 9, **9**, 11, 13–15, **14–15**, 17, 43, **44**, 45–65, **46**, 47, **53**, **54**, **58**, **60**, **63**, **65**, 87, 88, 91, 96, **97**, 117, **118–119**, 124
Beckham, Romeo, 8, 62
"Beckham Rule," 8
Beckham, Ted, 43, 47
Beckham, Victoria, 8, 59, 62, **63**, 64
Belgium, 10
Bend It Like Beckham (movie), 7, 113, 132
Benfica, 123
Best, George, 39, **40**, 42, 43, 93, 121, 124, **125**
bicycle kick. See overhead kick
Big Count, 27

Bobby Charlton Soccer School, 117
Bolivia, 115, 116
Bosman, Jean Marc, 124
Bosman Rule, 124–126
Bradenton Academy, 119, 120
Brazil, 27, 30–31, 100
Busby, Matt, 40–41, 42, 126
Butt, Nicky, **47**, 49, 51
Byrne, Roger, 41

C

calf trap, 90
Canada, 10, 24, 120
Cantona, Eric, 39, 43, 126
Carbajal, Antonio, 126
cards, yellow and red, 82, **83**, **84–85**
Carlos, Alberto, 126
Carlos, Roberto, 57
Carragher, Jamie, 117
catenaccio, 28
The Cauldron, 17
Celtic F.C., 138
Centennial Firm, 17
center-back, 69
Charles, John, 126
Charles, Prince, 62
Charlton, Bobby, **18**, **40**, 41–42, 47, 126–127
Charlton, Jack, **18**, 127
Chastain, Brandi, **108**, 109, 110, 112, 113, 127
chest trap, 90
Chicago Bulls, 57
Chicago Fire, 16–17
Chicago Magic, 119
China, 106, 107–109
Chivas USA, 16–17
Clinton, Chelsea, 107
Clinton, President Bill, 107
Club Deportivo Guadalajara, 17
Cohen, George, **21**
college soccer, 113, 120–121
Collina, Pierluigi, 127
Colorado Rapids, 16–17
Columbus Crew, 16–17
control of ball, 90–91
Corinthians, 99
corner kick, 72
Crew Union Local 103, 17
cross pass, 94
Cruise, Tom, 59–61
Cruyff, Johan, 91, 121, 127, 129

D

Dalglish, Kenny, 127
Dallas Cowboys, 34

David Beckham Academy, 117, **118–119**
David Beckham Predator Pulse, 61
Davies, John Henry, 35, 38
Davis, Rick, 127
D.C. United, 16–17, 123
Dean, William (Dixie), 129
defenders, 69, 70, 99
Dempsey, Clint, 117
Designated Player Rule, 8
Di Stefano, Alfredo, 129
Didi, 30, 129
diving, 100–103
Donovan, Landon, 119, **128**, 129
Double, the, 51, 55
dribbling, **73**, 92–93, **92–93**

E

Edwards, Duncan, 41, 137
Egerov, Igor, **66**
Elizabeth II, Queen, 20, **21**
Ellis, William Webb, 67
Empire Supporters, 17
England, **18**, 20–21, 27
English Premier League, 13, 43, 123, 126, 129, 137
Eton, 67–68
European Cup, 41–42, 55, 57, 126, 127, 129, 138
European Player of the Year, 136, 139
Eusebio, 129
Evani, Alberigo, **80–81**
Everest, Timothy, 62
Everton F.C., 129, 137

F

FA Cup, 34, 40, 52, **53**, 55, 126, 129
FA Youth Cup, 50
fair play, 99–103
Falklands War, 52
fan groups, 17
fashion, 62–64
Fawcett, Joy, 110, **112**
F.C. Dallas, 16–17
F.C. Delco, 119
F.C. Toronto, 16–17
F.C. Porto, 76
Ferguson, Alex, 43, 49, 50, 51, 52, 55, 56–57, 129
Fedération Internationale de Football Association (FIFA), 68, 105
Figo, Luis, 57
first touch, 90, 94
fitness, 103
football (American), 11, 12

Football Association (FA), 34
Football League, 39–40, **40**, 52, 55, 126, 134, 136
forwards, 69, 70
Foudy, Julie, 110
Foulkes, Billy, **40**
fouls, 75, 76, 77, 78, 81, 82, **83**, **84–85**, 100
Fowler, Robbie, 117
France, **22**, 27
Fraser, Ian, **74**
free kick, 78, 87, 88
free kick, indirect, 78–79, 81
fullback, 69
Fuller, Simon, 8

G
Galácticos, 57, 58
Garber, Don, 11
Gardner, Paul, 15
Garrincha (of Brazil), 30, 93, 129
Gascoigne, Paul, 59, 130, **130**
Germany, 13, 19–20, 24, 27, 105
Gerrard, Steven, 117
Giggs, Ryan, 39, **47**, 49, 50, 93, 117, 130
Gillette, 7
girls in soccer, 105–113, 117, 131
goal kick, 72, 88
goal scoring, 12, **29**, **32**
goalkeeper, 69, 70, 75, 78, 81, 103, 139
Gone in Sixty Seconds (movie), 132
Gregg, Harry, 41
Gullit, Ruud, 131

H
hairstyles, **60**, 61–62
Hamm, Mia, 110, **111**, 113, 131
Hansen, Alan, 51, 132
Hargreaves, Owen, 131
Harrison, Eric, 117
head, use of, 91, 96, **97**
history of soccer, 67
Hoddle, Glenn, 52–55, 131
Holland, 12, 28, 30
Holmes, Katie, 59
Hooper, Charmaine, 112
Houston Dynamo, 16–17
Hurst, Geoff, 131

I,J
The Inferno, 17
Italy, **22**, 27
It's Not About the Bra (book), 109
James, Alex, 131
Jerry Maguire (movie), 59

Johnson, Eddie, 119
Johnstone, Jimmy, 93
Jones, Vinnie, 132
Jordan, Michael, 57
juggling, 91
Juventus, 126

K
Kaka (of Brazil), 30
Kansas City Wizards, 16–17
Kays, the, 49
Kempes, Mario, 132
kicking techniques, 87–90
Kissinger, Henry, 13
Klinsmann, Jurgen, 132

L
La Liga, 57, 58
Lalas, Alexi, 11
Laos, 114
Law, Denis, **40**, 42, 43, 132
Law 18, 76
Laws of the Game, 27, 68, 75. *See also* rules of soccer
Leeds United, 126
Legion 1908, 17
Leiweke, Tim, 11
Lilly, Kristine, 110, 112, 132
Lineker, Gary, 132
Liverpool Academy, 117
Liverpool F.C., 10, 39, 117, 127, 137
Ljungberg, Hanna, **104**
Lock, Stock and Two Smoking Barrels (movie), 132
long pass, 94
Los Angeles Galaxy, 7, 8, **9**, 11, 15, 16–17, 57, 58, 59, 61, **79**, 129
The Loyalists, 17

M
MacMillan, Shannon, 106, 110, 112
Major League Baseball, 12
Major League Soccer, 7, 9, 11, 12, 15, 79, 120, 123
Maldini, Cesare, 88
Maldini, Paolo, 88, 89, 134
Manchester Brewery Company, 35
Manchester United, 9, **32**, 33–43, **35**, **40**, 45, 48–49, 50, 51, 52, 55, 56–57, 59, 61, 117, 124, 126, 129, 130, 132, 136, 137
Mansley, Paul, 64
Maradona, Diego, 13, 70, 91, 93, 121, 129, 133, 134
marking, 99
Matthäus, Lothar, 134

Matthews, Stanley, 134
McClaren, Steve, 58
Mean Machine (movie), 132
Mellgren, Dagny, 112
Messi, Lionel, 93
Mexico, 23, 24
Michels, Rinus, 121, 134
midfielders, 69, 70
Midnight Riders, 17
Milbrett, Tiffeny, 110
Milla, Roger, 135
Monaco (soccer team), 131
Moore, Bobby, 135
Morales, Evo, 116
Motorola, 7
Mourinho, José, 13
movement, 95–96, 100–101
Müller, Gerd, 135
Munich Clock, 42
Munich crash, 41–42, 43
Mussolini, Benito, 136

N
National Collegiate Athletic Association (NCAA), 120
National Football League, 12
Neville, Gary, **47**, 49, 50, 51, 59, 70, 117
Neville, Phil, 49, 51
New England Revolution, 16–17
Newsweek (magazine), 109
New York Cosmos, **122**, 124, 126, 127, 135
New York Knicks, 34
New York Yankees, 34
Newcastle United, 53, 137
Newton Heath LYR, 34–35
Nielsen, Kim Milton, 52, **54**
Nomads, 119
North America, 115–17
North American Soccer League, 124
Northern Ireland, 124
Norway, 105, 106
numbering system, 70

O
offside, 79–81
Old Trafford, **36–37**, 38, 42, 43, 48
Olympic Games, 26, 105–107, 123, 132
"one-on-one," **102**
one-two-pass, 94
Overbeck, Carla, 110
overhead kick, **89**, 89–90
Owen, Michael, 59, **89**, 117
Oxford University, 138

P

Parlow, Cindy, 110, **112**
Passarella, Daniel, 135
passing, 93–94
Pelé, 13, 30, **31**, 70, 90, 121, **122**, 124, 126, 127, 129, 134, 135, 136, 139
penalty area, 78
penalty kick, **44**, 78, **106–107**, 107–109
penalty shoot-out, 78, **80–81**, **106–107**, 107–109
Pepsi, 7
Philip, Prince, 20
Planicka, Frantisek, 135
Platini, Michel, 136
playing field, **71**
"Posh Spice," 8, 59
positions, 69
power kick, 88, 94
Pozzo, Vittorio, 136
Predator Mania, **65**
Premier League. See English Premier League
Preston North End, 50, 51, 58
Prinz, Birgit, 112
protective equipment, 103
push pass, 94
Puskas, Ferenc, 136

R

Ramsey, Alf, 20, 136
Raul (of Spain), 57
Real Madrid, 8, 9, 11, 17, 34, 57, 58, 129, 136
Real Salt Lake, 16–17
Real SoCal, 120
Red Bull New York, 15, 16–17
red card, **54**, 82, **84–85**
Red Patch Boys, 17
Red Star Belgrade, **35**, 41
referees, 52, **54**, **66**, 70, 75, 76, 78, 82, **83**, **84–85**, 100, 127
Ridgeway Rovers, 47
Riot Squad/Galaxians, 17
Romario (of Brazil), 30, 136
Ronaldinho, 30, 93, 136
Ronaldo (of Brazil), 9, 30, 57, 136–137
Ronaldo, Cristiano, 43, 137
Rooney, Wayne, 43, 137
Rose Bowl stadium, **80–81**, 107
Rugby School, 67
rules of soccer, 67–69, 76. See also Laws of the Game
Russia, **97**

S

salaries, 34
samba, 30–31
Sanchez, Hugo, 137
Santa Clara University, 113
Santos, 126
Schmeichel, Peter, 137
scholarships, 120–121
Scholes, Paul, 49, 51, 117
scoring, 69, 70
Scotland, 24
Screaming Eagles/Barra Brava, 17
Scurry, Briana, **106–107**, 109, 110
Section 8, 17
Seton Hall University, 113
Shankly, Bill, 137
Shearer, Alan, 59, 137
shin guards, 103
shirt colors, 10, 69. See also uniform colors
Simeone, Diego, 52, **54**
Sindelar, Matthias, 138
Sissi, 112
Smith, Kelly, **92–93**, 113
Sobrero, Kate, 110
soccer academies, 117–20
soccer clothes, 61, 64, 103
Soccer Development Academy, 119–120
Socrates (of Brazil), 30
Solar F.C., 119
Solskjaer, Ole Gunnar, 39
songs, 39
South Africa, 24
South America, 121
space, making, 95–96
Spanish Cup, 57
Spencer, Lady Diana, 62
Spice Girls, 8, 59
sportsmanship, 99–103
Spurs. See Tottenham Hotspur
Stade de France, 24, **25**
Stafford, Harry, 35
Stallone, Sylvester, 138
Stewart, Rod, 138
Strachan, Gordon, 61
Stretford End, 38
styles of soccer, 27–31
substitutes, 68
Sullivan, Neil, 45
Sun Wen, 112
Super Bowl, 12, 26
Sweden, 98, 106
systems of play, 70

T

tackling, **95**, 98–99
Taffarel, Claudio, **80–81**
Taylor, Tommy, 41
televised sports, 12
Texian Army/El Batallon, 17
thigh trap, 90
through pass, 94
throw-in, 70–71, 72, **74**, 76
ticket sales, 17
Toronto Maple Leafs, 34
Total Football, 28, 30, 127, 131, 134
Tottenham Hotspur, 9–10, 48, 49, 131
trapping the ball, 90–91
turns, 91

U,V

UEFA Champions League, 13
uniform colors, 23, 27, 33. See also shirt colors
United States, 10, 11–13, 24, 28, 105, 106–109, 112–113, 120
United States Soccer Federation (USSF), 119
Uruguay, 27
Valderrama, Carlos, 138
van Nistelrooy, Ruud, 90
Venables, Terry, **46**, 48
Victory (movie), 90, 138

W

wall (of defenders),78, **79**, 87
wall pass, 94
Walt Disney, 7
Weah, George, 138
weather conditions, 28, 30
websites, 33
Wembley Stadium, 20
Wen, Sun. See Sun Wen
White Hart Lane stadium, 48
Wilson, Ray, **18**
Wimbledon Football Club, 45, 132
W-League, 113
women in soccer, 105–113, 120, 123, 131
Women's European Cup, **10**
Women's Soccer Initiative (WSI), 113
Women's Soccer Olympics (1996), **112**
Women's United Soccer Association (WUSA), 112
Women's World Cup, 105–109, 123, 132
Women's World Cup (1999), 107–109, **108**, 112, 127